MMXVII

THE PROPHETIC 2017 ALMANAC

BILL JENKINS

Copyright © 2016
Church of ACTS Publishing
All rights reserved.

The Prophetic Almanac 2017

By Pastor Bill Jenkins

ALL RIGHTS RESERVED
No part of this book may be reproduced, transmitted or copied by any means, electronically or photo duplicated without permission of the author. Unless otherwise noted, all scripture quotations are from the King James Version of the Bible.

Manufactured in the
United States of America
ISBN #978-1-5323-2096-5

Published by
Church of ACTS Publishing
Indianapolis, Indiana
Visit the author's websites at
www.churchofacts.org
www.destinylandcc.org

TABLE OF CONTENTS
MMXVII

INTRODUCTION — 1

CHAPTER I — 5

    Calendar for 2017

CHAPTER II — 9

    What to Watch for in 2017

CHAPTER III — 19

    Fun Facts for Seventeen

CHAPTER IV — 25

    Prophetic Vision for 2017

CHAPTER V — 41

    Old Testament Speak to Me - Part 1
    Genesis – 2ND Samuel

CHAPTER VI — 69

Old Testament Speak to Me – Part 2
1 Kings – Ezekiel

CHAPTER VII — 97

New Testament Speak to Me

CHAPTER VIII — 111

Spiritual Forecast for All 50 States

CHAPTER IX — 171

Characteristics of 17th Day People

CHAPTER X — 179

Bible by the Numbers

CHAPTER XI — 187

Scriptures for Success for 2017

CHAPTER XII — 197

Journal

CONCLUSION — 205

INTRODUCTION

Here it is, The Annual Prophetic Almanac 2017! Last year's edition was such a great success. We were able to get the heart of God out to millions through TV, radio interviews, and through the message of the book. So much revelation has proven to come to pass on a daily basis, from interesting facts, to Bible passages, to specific words for individuals, as well as states. The New Prophetic Almanac for 2016 was truly a vehicle God used to share advanced information with His children.

Here are some of the things we saw come to pass from the Prophetic Almanac 2016:

- Tennessee was in the headlines quite a bit including that the lawmakers voted the Bible as the state's official book.
- The University of Tennessee won the Outback Bowl. On January 1, 2016, Outback Steakhouse celebrated their winning by giving free Bloomin' Onions to all customers that day.
- The 50th Super Bowl halftime show promoted the vision for the year with their display of *LOVE*.

- In July of 2016, we saw the damages from the Texas state Prophetic Word… *"Beware of riots in Dallas."*
- People to watch for included both Donald Trump and Hillary Clinton, who won their political party nominations.
- It was declared that something big would come from Chicago in the fall and the Chicago Cubs broke their 108 year losing streak and claimed the 2016 World Series title.

My hope, with The Prophetic Almanac 2017, is to once again provide you with knowledge concerning upcoming natural and supernatural events for the entire year. I also desire for this book to inspire and educate you in the wisdom of the Word of God. I always want it to be a fun and enjoyable read, but it's my prayer that as the prophetic revelation flows throughout this book, you will allow God to give you divine insight and direction to fulfill your destiny in 2017. I have spent hundreds of hours attempting to produce a book that will not just move the hearts of people but will release the heart of God for this year. As you read The Prophetic Almanac 2017, remember this, it is written to give you information, inspiration, and divine revelation to set you up for success. Pay attention to the small devotions that are given through every book of the Bible that has a chapter 17. Look at the word for your particular state, and make a daily habit to pray blessings over the place you live. Share the fun facts with others. This will give them a curiosity that will cause an interest for them to know God more, and study the Word for themselves.

This is a year that God is truly releasing a once-in-a-lifetime opportunity to RESET things in our lives. Seventeen, in part, is connected to having one season end and, at the same time, having another season begin. It's important to make sure we are prepared, from the inside out, for God to move things back to its original position. We have to desire more than "Cosmetic Christianity", and have a greater desire to minimize the distance between us and the Lord. Seventeen in Hebrew means, "To shine upon and give light." God is shedding light upon things that need to change in our lives. This will prepare us to hit that "Reset" button in our lives. We don't want a new paint job on a vehicle with a bad engine. The words of Ephesians 5:14 are a prophetic wake up call to the world:

"Wherefore he saith, Awake thou that sleepest, and arise from the dead, and Christ shall give thee light."

No matter who you are, or what you've done that you are running away from, this is your year to REWRITE the story of your life. OMG!! Are you serious? Absolutely! Don't turn a deaf ear to the words of this book, for they are a revelation from God Himself, to you, to reveal His awesome plans in 2017.

> *"For I know the thoughts that I think toward you, saith the Lord, thoughts of peace, and not of evil, to give you an expected end."*
> Jeremiah 29:11

Seventeen is a positive Biblical number, and will release REVIVAL in our hearts that can spread to other people. The days of political correctness are over, but it's more important than ever to hold ourselves personally accountable to the commands of the Word of God. I'm looking forward to what this year brings so let's jump in, and receive the plan of God for 2017.

CHAPTER I

2017 Calendar

JANUARY

1st - New Year's Day
6th - Epiphany
16th - Martin Luther King Day
16th - Civil Rights Day
20th - Inauguration Day
28th - Chinese New Year

FEBRUARY

1st - National Freedom Day
2nd - Groundhog Day
5th - Super Bowl 51
3rd - National Wear Red Day
12th - Lincoln's Birthday
14th - Valentine's Day
15th - Susan B. Anthony's Birthday
19th - NBA All-Star Game
20th - President's Day
26th - Daytona 500

MARCH

1st - Ash Wednesday

3rd - Employee Appreciation Day
11th - Purim
12th - Daylight Savings Time Starts
17th - St. Patrick's Day

APRIL

1st - April Fool's Day
3rd - Men's NCAA Basketball Championship
9th - Palm Sunday
10th - Passover begins
13th - Maundy Thursday
13th - Thomas Jefferson's Birthday
14th - Good Friday
16th - Easter
17th - Patriot's Day
18th - Tax Day
26th - Administrative Assistant Day

MAY

1st - Loyalty Day
4th - National Day of Prayer
5th - Cinco de Mayo
6th - National Nurses Day
6th - Kentucky Derby
14th - Mother's Day
20th - Armed Forces Day
25th - National Missing Children's Day
28th - Indianapolis 500

29th - Memorial Day
30th - Shavuot

JUNE

4th - Pentecost
6th - D-Day
11th - Trinity Sunday
14th - Flag Day
18th - Father's Day

JULY

4th - Independence Day
11th - MLB All-Star Game
23rd - Parent's Day

AUGUST

7th - Purple Heart Day
14th - Victory Day
19th - National Aviation Day
21st - Senior Citizens Day
26th - Women's Equality Day

SEPTEMBER

4th - Labor Day

10th - National Grandparent's Day
15th - National POW/MIA Recognition Day
20th - Rosh Hashanah
22nd - Native Americans' Day
29th - Yom Kippur

OCTOBER

2nd - Child Health Day
9th - Columbus Day
16th - Boss' Day
31st - Halloween

NOVEMBER

5th - Daylight Savings Time Ends
11th - Veteran's Day
23rd - Thanksgiving Day
24th - Black Friday
27th - Cyber Monday

DECEMBER

7th - Pearl Harbor Remembrance Day
12th - Chanukah/Hanukkah Begins
24th - Christmas Eve
25th - Christmas Day
31st - New Year's Eve

CHAPTER II

What to Watch for in 2017

The Lord will often put specific people, places, dates, or things on my heart just to keep an eye out for. I feel He usually does it to get me to begin to pray for that person, place, or situation. I don't always understand why He may at first, but by the end of the year, I feel He has shown me the reason. These are things that may seem small, but He has put them on my heart for 2017. Many times it is just confirmation to me that I still hear His voice and that I need to listen to it and trust. Keep an eye out for these specific things this year. Begin to lift them up in prayer. Pay attention to how much you will begin to hear about these things over the next year.

Geographical Places to Watch in 2017
- Cuba
- North Korea
- Italy
- Atlantic Ocean
- Central America
- Canada

Vegetable for 2017
Corn

Fruit of the Spirit for 2017
Goodness

Gift of the Spirit for 2017
Gifts of Healing

Biblical Characters to Study in 2017
- Men = Noah
- Women = Esther
- Youth = Joseph

Animal of the Year
Rooster

A rooster is a male chicken. They are only mentioned in the New Testament. They were primarily used for three specific reasons:

1. Watching
2. Warning
3. Warring

Roosters were the guard dogs of the New Testament. They would warn of impending storms or neighborhood disturbances. They were also used in fighting, as the Romans used them, as a form of gambling, and entertainment. Roosters are connected to Peter's betrayal of Jesus in Mark

14:30. Here are some positive and negative characteristics of roosters that should cause us to be aware of our own behavior and actions in 2017:

Characteristics of Roosters

Positive	Negative
• Social Animals	• Self-Centered
• Compassionate	• Overly Confident
• Physically Strong	• Talkative
• Very Healthy	• Moody
• Born Leader	• Prideful
• Hard-Working	• Vain
• Brave	• Hot Tempered
• Loyal & Devoted	• Always Busy
• Observant/Watchful	• Self-Promoters
• Fighters	• Independent
• Honest	• Attention Seeker
• Charming	• Overly Ambitious
• Recover Quickly from Illness & Rejection	• Emotionally Sensitive

Scripture for 2017

2 Chronicles 20:17
"*Ye shall not need to fight in this battle: set yourselves, stand ye still, and see the salvation of the Lord with you, O Judah and Jerusalem: fear*

not, nor be dismayed; tomorrow go out against them: for the Lord will be with you."

State for 2017
Ohio

17 People to Watch for in 2017
1. Arnold Schwarzenegger, Celebrity
2. Stephen King, Author
3. Paul Ryan, Speaker of the House
4. Lady Gaga, Singer
5. Adam Sandler, Actor
6. Tom Cruise, Actor
7. Kevin Durant, NBA
8. Pamela Anderson, Celebrity
9. Tom Brady, NFL
10. Mark Burnett, Producer
11. Amy Poehler, Actress
12. Britney Spears, Singer
13. Spike Lee, Director
14. Paula Abdul, Singer/Dancer
15. Sean Combs, Singer/ Businessman
16. Daniel Radcliffe, Actor
17. Mike Pence, Vice President

Colors for 2017
- Salmon
- Tropical Blue

Snack for 2017
Almonds & Pistachio Nuts (Genesis 43:11)
(If you count the letters in almonds & pistachios it equals 17)

17 Words with 17 Letters to Watch for in 2017
1. Authoritativeness
2. Conscientiousness
3. Characterizations
4. Constitutionalism
5. Declassifications
6. Extraterrestrials
7. Inappropriateness
8. Indistinguishably
9. Interconnectivity
10. Misappropriations
11. Opportunistically
12. Ultraconservative
13. Tenderheartedness
14. Adventuresomeness
15. Unconventionality
16. Videoconferencing
17. Counterterrorists

Bible Story for 2017
Noah's Ark

Bible Book for 2017
Titus

Numbers to Watch for in 2017

Bible numbers not only enrich our spiritual understanding but also help us to discern the true intent of God for a particular passage of scripture. Here are some numbers to watch for in 2017. These numbers are not given for you to play the lottery but for you to understand God's plans more clearly for this year:

1 = Beginnings
2 = Agreement
3 = Completion/Closure
7 = Perfection
10 = Lawful
18 = Bondage
20 = Judgment
23 = Greatness
41 = Personal Victory
90 = Destiny
100 = Promises Fulfilled

Look for new beginnings. As you walk in agreement, God will bring closure to your past. You are perfected by understanding and applying His truths to your life. It will bring the freedom from bondage you have been looking for in your life. There is no condemnation in the Lord, only greatness to achieve personal victory and fulfill the destiny He has promised.

17 Movies to Watch for 2017

1. XXX 3: The Return of Xander Cage (January)
2. Fifty Shades Darker (February)
3. Power Rangers (March)
4. Logan: Wolverine 3 (March)
5. Fast 8 (April)
6. Baywatch (May)
7. Pirates of the Caribbean: Dead Men Tell No Tales (May)
8. Wonder Woman (June)
9. Transformers (June)
10. The Mummy (June)
11. Despicable Me 3 (June)
12. War for the Planet of the Apes (July)
13. The Hitman's Bodyguard (August)
14. American Made (September)
15. Justice League (November)
16. Thor: Ragnarok (November)
17. Star Wars: Episode VIII (December)

When the year of 2017 comes to an end, it will be defined as a year of:
- Opportunities
- Weather Related Mysteries
- Beginnings
- Social Unrest

- Personal Victory
- Closure
- Discovery
- Animation
- Space Exploration

Hurricane Names for 2017
Watch specifically for Emily, Maria, Philippe, and Sean:

1. Arlene
2. Bret
3. Cindy
4. Don
5. Emily
6. Franklin
7. Gert
8. Harvey
9. Irma
10. Jose
11. Katia
12. Lee
13. Maria
14. Nate
15. Ophelia
16. Philippe
17. Rina
18. Sean
19. Tammy
20. Vince
21. Whitney

17 Prophetic Dates to Watch for in 2017

Keep your spiritual ears and eyes open for something significant and even life-changing to happen on these specific dates in 2017:

1. Thursday, January 5, 2017
2. Friday, January 20, 2017

3. Wednesday, February 8, 2017
4. Friday, February 17, 2017
5. Monday, March 6, 2017
6. Sunday, April 2, 2017
7. Tuesday, April 18, 2017
8. Wednesday, May 3, 2017
9. Saturday, June 10, 2017
10. Friday, July 7, 2017
11. Monday, August 21, 2017
12. Wednesday, September 13, 2017
13. Friday, September 29, 2017
14. Thursday, October 5, 2017
15. Monday, October 23, 2017
16. Tuesday, November 14, 2017
17. Saturday, December 16, 2017

17 Predictions for 2017

- A new unknown disease to be in the headlines
- Look for Queen Elizabeth's reign to end in 2017
- Social unrest will create great riots and Civil War-like divisions
- Skin diseases to dramatically rise
- Teams that wear blue to win championships
- Massive earthquakes and hurricanes in usual and unusual places in America
- Ohio will be in the news for a large political scandal

- Global power outages
- A political assassination to occur in 2017
- Look for sport figures who wear the #17 to have a huge year
- Pay attention to global terrorism in Italy and Ireland
- Lone-wolf terrorists to network with one another to develop a destructive plan in the heart of America to be exposed
- Watch the oceans for unusual patterns
- Other European nations will exit the European Union like Britain
- Financial chaos in October will hit the world
- New planets will be discovered
- Large scale food shortage will occur in the world

CHAPTER III

FUN FACTS FOR SEVENTEEN

Biblical Facts

- Rehoboam, Solomon's son, reigned for 17 years (930-913) in 1 Kings 14
- In Ezekiel 45:13, a sixth part of wheat and barley is approximately 17%
- 17 nations were represented at Pentecost in Acts 2:7-11
- Joseph was 17 when he was sold into slavery by his brothers in Genesis 37:2
- Jacob lived 17 years in Egypt in Genesis 47:28
- Jehoahaz, son of Jehu, reigned for 17 years in 2 Kings 13:1
- The 10 Commandments are explained over 17 verses in Exodus 20
- Daniel's seven beasts have seven heads and ten horns or 17 total parts
- In 1 Corinthians 13, the 17th mention of love comes in verse 13, where Paul declares love is the greatest gift

- Day of Atonement, or Yom Kippur, occurs on the tenth day of the seventh month of the Hebrew Calendar
- The book of James was written 17 years after the resurrection of Christ
- The books of 1 Corinthians and James have information from 17 Old Testament books
- 2 Samuel has 17,170 words in the entire book
- The flood started on the 17th day in Genesis 7:11
- Noah's Ark came to rest on Mount Ararat on the 17th day in Genesis 8:4
- Mount Ararat is approximately 17,000 feet tall
- When the disciples couldn't catch any fish, Jesus told them to cast the net on the right side of the boat in John 21. They caught 153 fish. If you add the numbers from one to seventeen you will get 153:
1+2+3+4+5+6+7+8+9+10+11+12+13+14+15+16+17 = 153
- Manna is mentioned in the Bible 17 times
- Psalm 83:6-11 contains a list of 17 enemies of Israel

- There are 17 plagues in the Bible:

10 Plagues of Egypt	7 Plagues of Last Days
1. Water turned to blood	1. Sores
2. Frogs	2. Sea turns to blood
3. Lice and Fleas	3. Rivers turn to blood
4. Flies	4. People burned by sun
5. Cattle die of disease	5. Darkness
6. Boils and Sores	6. River Euphrates dries up
7. Hail	7. Earthquakes
8. Locusts	
9. Darkness	
10. Death of firstborn	

- Judges 3:8 mentions the only name in the Bible containing 17 letters, Chushanrishathaim. He was king of Mesopotamia who oppressed Israel in the generation that followed Joshua. His name means "to double the darkness"

- 17 Books of the Bible begin with a number:
  - 1 Samuel
  - 2 Samuel
  - 1 Kings
  - 2 Kings
  - 1 Chronicles
  - 2 Chronicles
  - 2 Thessalonians
  - 1 Timothy
  - 2 Timothy
  - 1 Peter
  - 2 Peter
  - 1 John

- 1 Corinthians
- 2 Corinthians
- 1 Thessalonians
- 2 John
- 3 John

Entertainment Facts

- There were eight movies from the past that were set in 2017:
    - Barb Wire (1996)
    - Cherry 2000 (1988)
    - Click (2006)
    - The Running Man (1987)
    - Fortress (1992)
    - Surrogates (2009)
    - Thirst (1979)
    - Terminator Genesys (2015)
- There is a magazine for teenagers called "Seventeen"
- 17 Songs with 17 in the title:
    1. Edge of Seventeen – Stevie Nicks (1982)
    2. At Seventeen – Janis Ian (1975)
    3. Seventeen – Winger (1988)
    4. Seventeen – Tim McGraw (2009)
    5. 17 – Avril Lavigne (2013)
    6. 17 – Kings of Leon (2008)
    7. Seventeen – Mat Kearney (2011)
    8. 17 Again – Eurythmics (1996)
    9. 17 – Cross Canadian Ragweed (2002)
    10. 17 Days – Prince (1993)
    11. Seventeen – Ladytron (2002)
    12. Sexy & 17 – The Stray Cats (1983)
    13. 17 – Youth Lagoon (2002)

14. What a Nice Way to Turn 17 – The Crystals (1962)
15. 17 Crimes – AFI (2013)
16. Seventeen Forever – Metro Station (2008)
17. Damn You Seventeen – Lady Antebellum (2014)

Historical Facts

- Ohio became the 17th state in the United States in 1803
- July 17th is Constitution Day in South Korea
- Italy considers 17 to be an unlucky number, while Ireland considers 17 to be a number of celebration
- The last mission to the moon was Apollo 17
- The French Revolution occurred in 1789 (8+9 =17, so you have two - 17's)
- Beethoven wrote 17 quartets, while Shakespeare wrote 17 comedies

Political Facts

- The White House is located between 15th and 17th Street in Washington, D.C.
- The 17th President was Andrew Johnson who was Vice President for Abraham Lincoln and took over when he was assassinated. Andrew Johnson was the first

President to be impeached for firing a cabinet member
- The 17th Amendment to the U.S. Constitution is the Direct Election of U.S. Senators

General Facts

- The fear of the number 17 is called "heptakaidekaphobia"
- Most people consider the tongue to have 17 muscles
- A heptadecagon has 17 sides
- Twenty-Seventeen in Greek is, epiphaino, which means, "to shine upon or give light"
- The atomic number of chlorine is 17
- It takes approximately 17 muscles in your face to smile
- The Roman numeral for 17 is MMXVII

CHAPTER IV

PROPHETIC VISION

The number "seventeen" or "seventeenth" is mentioned a combined total of 18 times in the King James and New International Version of the Bible. It's from these verses that we can gain an understanding of its meaning and allow the secrets to reveal a prophetic plan for our lives.

> *"The secret things belong unto the Lord our God: but those things which are revealed belong unto us and to our children forever, that we may do all the words of this law."* Deuteronomy 29:29

> *"It is the glory of God to conceal a matter, but the glory of Kings is to search out a matter."* Proverbs 25:2

Let's use this study as a way to show the Lord our spiritual hunger and reveal our desire to know Him more. Let's prove to God that we want to reign with Him. Searching takes time and involves work. It suggests a thorough investigation and not a casual seeking. We must stop playing games by saying all the right things and then not putting them into practice in our lives. God will reveal His will to us for 2017 through His Word, but let's respect Him enough to apply it in our daily lives.

The 18 references to the number seventeen reveal God's four-fold purpose for our lives in 2017.

Four-Fold Plan for 2017

1. **Reset**
2. **Divine Healing**
3. **Total Victory**
4. **Revealing**

The vision of 2016 was all about our responsibility to God. He required us to focus on four things that would set us up for success:

1. Love
2. Maturity
3. Marriage and Family
4. Personal Dominion

To whatever degree we took those things seriously and applied them to our lives, is to the degree He will release His promise to us. The vision for 2017 is all about God revealing Himself in response to our obedience. If you didn't increase in love by drawing a circle around yourself and allowing personal dominion to begin in your heart, don't blame God if you fail. If you weren't interested in growing up and focusing in on your family, don't get jealous when others have the favor of God bestowed upon them.

Favor isn't fair!! It comes to those who are implementing the truths of God's Word and His prophet's revelations to their lives.

> *"...Have faith in the Lord your God and you will be upheld; have faith in his prophets and you will be successful."* 2 Chronicles 20:20 (NIV)

RESET

The number one reference to the use of seventeen in the Bible is in direct reference to a resetting in our lives. It is where one season ends and another begins. Two kings in the Old Testament had their reign come to an end after 17 years. Jacob lived in Egypt for 17 years. Joseph had his family life come to an end at age 17. But, the biggest connection of all is how the flood in Genesis began on the 17th day of the month and how the Ark came to rest on Mt. Ararat, after the flood, on the 17th day of the following month. There was a resetting in the world.

A few months ago (May 2016), the Lord gave me a dream with a reset button. The edge was white while the button was red with white letters that said, "RESET." He said, "Are you ready?", and I said, "Ready for what?" The Lord said, "Are you ready to hit the reset button in your life? I am releasing a once-in-a-lifetime opportunity for My faithful people to reset their lives and rewrite their story." He also encouraged me to check my heart for any impurities. God doesn't want us to look good on the outside, while our hearts are a mess. He doesn't want "Cosmetic Christianity" to be a part of our lives. You shouldn't go paint a car when the engine doesn't run. He doesn't want us to hit a reset button as some gimmick that won't last. He wants us to be prepared for a release of His glory that will truly have the kind of impact that produces true change in us and others. To reset means, "To set again, to change the reading back to zero, to move something back to its original place and position" like a broken bone or a mileage odometer. It also refers to a stop watch or timing gun.

We may have failed badly in life up to this point. It might be something we have done to mess stuff up or something the devil has imposed upon us. Either way, that season has the potential to come to an end. You have allowed your past to dictate your feelings and determine your future long enough. This is a once-in-a-lifetime opportunity to let those things go, and get your heart right with God, so you can begin to have new doors open to rewrite the story of your life.

DIVINE HEALING

This is a year for divine healing to manifest in your life. It is for every area including emotional healing, marital healing, financial healing, but most of all, physical healing. There are 17 general diseases mentioned in the Bible. A disease is a sickness that affects part or the whole of your body. When you break the word disease down, you get "dis-ease" or "lack of ease". God wants to heal whatever has been unpleasant, painful, numb, nagging, annoying, or burdensome in your body. His plan is to fire and get rid of discomfort and disease. We have a promise of healing in Isaiah 53:4-5:

> *"Surely he hath borne our griefs, and carried our sorrows: yet we did esteem him stricken, smitten of God, and afflicted. But he was wounded for our transgressions, he was bruised for our iniquities: the chastisement of our peace was upon him; and with his stripes we are healed."*

Seventeen Diseases of the Bible

1. **Blindness:** Mark 8:22-25, John 9:1-7

    Blindness in the Old Testament was common because of blowing sand and unsanitary conditions. Now, it's hereditary or degeneration over time for the most part, although there are other causes. However the blindness occurred, whether total or partial, one eye or both, spiritual or physical, God is healing our eyes. Cataracts, glaucoma, dryness, retinitis, pigmentosa, farsighted, near-sighted, and macular degeneration will be healed in Jesus name.

2. **Baldness:** Deuteronomy 14:1, Isaiah 15:2

    I am ready to hear complaints about this one. LOL!! The Jews usually had thick hair on their head and face. Growing hair was not a problem. It was a source of pride, and shaving was forbidden. Israel's neighbors often shaved their head as a sign of mourning. I'm not saying that all baldness is bad. Nowadays, some make it a choice, while others do it as a sign of celebration. Others are forced because of radiation treatment. I'm referring to baldness that comes as a result of ringworm of the scalp. If you want to grow hair but can't, try laying your hands on your head and breaking any generational curses while also casting out that ringworm that's eating your hair potential.

3. **Hunchback & Bone Disease:** Luke 13:11, Matthew 15:31

Osteoporosis, brittle bones, rickets, and bad posture will be healed in the name of Jesus.

4. **Addictions:** Hebrews 12:1, Proverbs 20:1

   - Alcohol
   - Nicotine
   - Caffeine
   - Sugar
   - Food
   - Prescription Drugs
   - TV
   - Illegal Drugs
   - Pornography
   - Sexual sins
   - Chocolate

5. **Skin Problems:** Exodus 9:9-10, Job 2:7, Deuteronomy 28:27, 35

   Such as sunburns, itching, rashes, eczema, psoriasis, dry skin, and even boils. Boils are inward infections that manifest outwardly. Hezekiah and Job both dealt with boils. The sixth plague of the Egyptians was boils. God is healing skin issues.

6. **Deafness:** Mark 7:32-35, Matthew 12:22

   It may be partial or complete, one ear or both will be healed. I hear the Lord say, *"Be healed of ringing and discomfort in your ears."*

7. **Eating Disorders:** Ps 102:4, Ps 107:18

   Bulimia, anorexia, gluttony, improper eating, and malnutrition will be healed.

8. **Female Issues:** Matthew 9:20

   God healed a woman with an issue of blood, so He can heal you. Lumps in breast, irregular periods, cysts, barrenness, extreme PMS, loss of sexual desire, miscarriages, along with worry and fear have to go. Lay your hands on yourself and declare healing.

9. **Cancer & Leukemia and other Blood Diseases:** 2 Timothy 2:17

   Lupus, Sickle Cell Anemia, Hemophilia, AIDS, HIV, every type of cancer, and blood diseases we curse you and cover you in the precious name of Jesus Christ. Be healed!!

10. **Dumbness:** Mark 7:32, Acts 9:17

    Dumbness refers to behavior but also to the inability to speak or speak clearly. Stuttering, sarcasm, lying, cursing, criticism, gossip, negative speech, autism, ADD, and Alzheimer be healed. Lord, heal us all!!!

11. **Dwarfism:** Leviticus 21:20, Matthew 15:31

    Dwarfism is referring to improper growth of limbs. Dwarfism may be inherited or caused by chronic kidney disease or malformations of the heart. Physical normalcy was required of priests to perform priestly duties. Grow, and grow up.

12. **Spirit of Infirmity:** John 5:5

An infirmity is a physical weakness or defect. Allergies, hay fever arthritis, sinus problems, heartburn, colds, headaches, fevers, flu, ulcers, acne, back pain, and ear aches are all considered infirmities. Mary Magdalene was healed of demonic bondage and a spirit of infirmity in Luke 8:2. You too will be healed.

13. **Emerods/Tumors:** Deuteronomy 28:27

Any improper swelling in or on the body be healed in Jesus name.

14. **Dropsy:** Luke 14:2

Dropsy is an abnormal accumulation of serious fluid in the tissues of the body. It is usually a result of a faulty heart or diseased kidney. God is your healer.

15. **Seizures & Epilepsy:** Matthew 17:14-20

It is not God's will for you to deal with this any longer. All brain and body malfunctions will be healed.

16. **Accident Prone:** Acts 28:1-6

   Snake bites, spider bites, burning, cutting, car accidents, hitting of heads, choking on foods, falling down stairs, and all other accidents that cause pain are serious and shouldn't be taken lightly. Break that accident prone spirit over your life.

17. **Paralysis:** John 5:1-8, Acts 3:2

   Any problems in your nervous system will be healed.

This is a large biblical list of things God wants to heal you from in 2017. Don't take offense to ones I mentioned or those I missed. God is not *required* to heal us of things we bring upon ourselves; however, He *still can* do it. He is required to heal everything the devil imposes upon us.

> *"How God anointed Jesus of Nazareth with the Holy Ghost and with power: who went about doing good, and healing all that were oppressed of the devil; for God was with him."* Acts 10:38

TOTAL VICTORY

Seventeen symbolizes complete victory. It refers to the total overcoming of all hurts, habits, and hang-ups that have held us back from fulfilling our destiny. Jesus Christ gained victory over death, hell, and the grave when by the power of the Holy Spirit, He was resurrected on the Hebrew month of Nisan on the 17th day.

> *"But if the Spirit of him that raised up Jesus from the dead dwell in you, he that raised up Christ from the dead shall also quicken your mortal bodies by his Spirit that dwelleth in you."* Romans 8:11

In 2 Kings 13, Elisha is over 100 years of age and terminally ill. Israel is dwelling in tents, and things aren't looking very good for their future. Verse 5 declares God sent them a Savior and gave them a word to give them total victory. Israel's army had been reduced to 50 horseman, 10 chariots, and 10,000 soldiers. Syria had much more war power and could have easily destroyed them, but God was with Israel.

> *"And Elisha said unto him, Take bow and arrows. And he took unto him bow and arrows. And he said to the king of Israel, Put thine hand upon the bow. And he put his hand upon it: and Elisha put his hands upon the king's hands. And he said, Open the*

window eastward. And he opened it. Then Elisha said, Shoot. And he shot. And he said, The arrow of the Lord's deliverance, and the arrow of deliverance from Syria: for thou shalt smite the Syrians in Aphek, till thou have consumed them." 2 Kings 13:15-17

The instructions were to take bows and arrows, and shoot out the east window until you have destroyed them. He didn't say, "Shoot until you defeat some, a few, or even a lot." "Shoot until you destroy them", is what he said. However, the king shot three times and was satisfied enough to quit in verse 18. The king's inability to properly listen and follow instructions not only angered the prophet but caused Israel to experience only limited victory. He could have annihilated Syria to the point they were utterly destroyed, never to be a bother again.

If you want victory, you have to listen, and obey the God-given instruction. You can have limited victory or total victory. It's your choice!!

When God wants to give a miracle, healing, deliverance, or complete victory in our lives, He always releases a Word first. It's what you do with that Word that determines whether you succeed or fail. The Word of 2017 is if you want total victory, then God wants total obedience.

REVEALING

Twenty-seventeen in the Greek is spelled, "epiphaino", and means, "to shine upon and give light". There are three main purposes of light:

1. Illuminates, John 1:4-5
2. Penetrates, John 8:12
3. Reveals, Luke 12:3

Light gives us the ability to clearly see things that can create damage and also causes us to see the beautiful things in life we might otherwise miss. It doesn't take a lot of light to penetrate darkness. Darkness gives way to light. However, the main purpose of light, for this discussion, is to reveal. God is wanting to reveal His secrets and give us greater revelation than we have ever had.

He is also expecting us to deal with our personal issues that still have a grip on our lives. 2017 is a year where if you don't deal with those private sins, then God will deal with them by exposing and shedding light on our inner darkness.

> *"For every one that doeth evil hateth the light, neither cometh to the light, lest his deeds should be reproved."* John 3:20

> *"He that covereth his sins shall not prosper: but whoso confesseth and forsaketh them shall have mercy."* Proverbs 28:13

"For ye were sometimes darkness, but now are ye light in the Lord: walk as children of light:" Ephesians 5:8

Darkness conceals, light reveals. God is exposing things that we are unwilling to deal with because He loves us and wants us free. God reveals to heal. Galatians 5:19-26 lists 17 works of the flesh that I believe are important for us to deal with and get delivered from in 2017:

17 Works of the Flesh

1. **Adultery** (moicheia) = sexual relations of a married person with someone other than your spouse

2. **Fornication** (porneia) = immoral sexual conduct and intercourse outside of marriage, includes pornographic books and movies

3. **Uncleanness** (akatharsia) = sexual sins, evil deeds including thoughts and desires of the heart

4. **Lasciviousness** (aselgeaia) = following one's passions and desires to the point of having no shame or public decency

5. **Idolatry** (eidololatria) = worship of spirits, persons, or graven images; also trust in any person, institution, or things as having equal or greater authority than God and His Word.

6. **Witchcraft** (pharmakeia) = sorcery, black magic, worship of demons, and use of drugs to produce spiritual experiences

7. **Hatred** (echthra) = intense, hostile intentions and acts

8. **Variance** (eris) = a struggle for superiority

9. **Emulations** (zelas) = resentfulness, envy of another's success

10. **Wrath** (thumos) = explosive anger or rage which flames into violent words and acts

11. **Strife** (eritheia) = selfish ambition and seeking of power

12. **Seditions** (dichostasia) = divisive teachings not supported by the Bible birthed in rebellion

13. **Heresies** (hairesis) = false teaching that causes division within the congregation into

selfish groups or cliques which destroy the unity of the church

14. **Envyings** (phthonos) = resentful dislike of another person who has something that one desires

15. **Murders** (phonos) = killing a person unlawfully and with malice

16. **Drunkenness** (methe) = impairing one's mental or physical control by alcoholic drink

17. **Revellings** (komos) = excessive feasting, a party spirit involving alcohol, drugs, and sex

Get things right, and have the best year of your Life

CHAPTER V

OLD TESTAMENT SPEAK TO ME – PART 1

Genesis 17
Rewrite Your Story

This is truly one of the most encouraging chapters in the Bible. It reveals God's ability to give us a second chance. In chapter 16, Abram and Sara almost messed everything up, but God is giving them another opportunity to make things right. God is once again renewing His covenant with Abram and insisting on the importance of human cooperation mixed with the sovereign power of God. Our destiny is decided by our ability to collaborate with God by doing our job and allowing God to do His. Abram's job was made clear in verse 1, "to walk blameless or perfect before God." Notice God said, "walk". He didn't say, "run and get ahead of God" or "crawl and get behind Him." In other words, be steady in your pace. God said to walk blameless or perfect. Blameless is about integrity and is more about progression than perfection.

God's promise wasn't based upon the perfection of man but the steady progression of man to put one foot in front of the other and move steadily towards Him to close the gap that Adam created when he sinned in the garden. God's job in response to man's obedience was to establish or set an everlasting covenant into motion to reassure His people that the great "I AM" will keep His promise.

Let's not forget Abram is 90 years old and is still being asked to be pliable in God's hands. As Abram did his part to right his wrong, to honor God with repentance, worship God, and cooperate with God, the Lord changed his name in verse 5 to Abraham.

Abram = Exalted Father

Abraham = Father of a Multitude

He was beginning to rewrite his story or *history*. Abram, who was a common and weak man, became Abraham, the father of the world. WOW!! Abraham's story was being rewritten. Then God released five blessings to reassure Abraham that God is a promise keeper.

5 Promises of God

1. I will make you exceedingly fruitful, v. 23

What God promised to Adam and Noah is again being reinforced. Not just fruitful, but exceedingly fruitful. The word exceedingly means, "to the extreme degree; way beyond the norm". Although others had messed up and even Abram had messed up, God's message not only remained the same, but it increased His desire and enthusiasm to keep His covenant.

2. I will make nations of you, and kings will come forth from you, v. 24

God is promising Abraham to give him a great quality of persons and not just a bunch of unqualified people. He is giving him a community of people composed of the best of every nationality and tribe. They will rule righteously and become kings after God's own heart. God also promised it would eventually culminate in Jesus being the King of Kings.

3. I will establish My covenant between Me and you and your descendants, v. 25

God is promising to establish a covenant that will be eternal. God is a God of longevity. He isn't a fickle God. God's covenant with Abraham promised that he would leave a legacy to his children, grandchildren, and beyond.

4. I will give you and your descendants the land as an everlasting possession, v. 26

God is giving land for them to own and live upon because He wants them to have possessions that belong to them. God is never against us owning things; He is only against things owning us.

5. I will be their God, v. 27

God is saving the best for last. He wants to bring increase, give us leaders after His own heart, release possessions that we can own, but He wants a relationship with us more than anything. He wants to be our God!!!

God is a forgiving and gracious God. Even though Abram and Sara tried to blow things in Genesis 16, God remained true to honoring His word. It should be refreshing to know that as long as we are trying to serve the Lord and remain right in His eyes, even our stupid decisions can't mess up the ultimate plan of God. God is bigger than our mistakes. God gave them a chance to make things right again. He gave them the opportunity to RESET and REWRITE as He renewed and revived His covenant. Allow God to be bigger than your mistakes in 2017.

~GOD IS BIGGER THAN YOUR PAST MISTAKES!!~

Exodus 17
Working Together: Winning Together

This is definitely one of my favorite chapters in the Bible. It's very symbolic of how working together means winning together. In a day where there has never been as much division as there is in our world now, we must learn our positions, and work together in unity.

Under the leadership of Moses, God delivered His people from the bondage of Egypt, but there were still battles to face on the way to the Promised Land. Israel came to a place called Rephidim, where the Amalekites, who were descendants of Esau, began to devise an attack upon God's people. According to Deuteronomy 25, the Amakelites would attack from the back side to take out the weak, the ill, the elderly, the young, and all the women. Moses' plan was to go and pray while he sent Joshua to fight. This was not a cowardly act on Moses' behalf, but a wise, shrewd, godly understanding of what each person is called to do in the Kingdom of God to achieve victory. He knew his best place was on the mountain praying while Joshua, who was born to war, was fighting in the valley.

Moses brought Aaron and Hur with him, and after a long period of prayer, Moses' hands and arms became tired. When he dropped his arms, the servants of God noticed that Joshua and his men began to lose the battle. Their discernment turned into action when they realized their part in the fight. They weren't supposed to replace Moses; they were supposed to support Moses. As they did their job by holding up Moses' hands, and Moses did his job by praying, Joshua had the strength to fight and win the battle in the valley. No one had a personal agenda, and no one tried to do something the Lord never enabled them to do. They were okay with who God made them to be, and they did their work with all their heart, and everyone enjoyed the victory. Here are some great lessons to learn to win in 2017.

Key Lessons to Learn Concerning our Gifts

1. **Know your gift**
2. **God is the giver of gifts**
3. **Every gift is uniquely designed to build the church, not the individual**
   The church is an orchestra, not a solo act.
4. **Gifts are to be used to keep you on the frontline and off the sideline**
5. **Show gratitude to God for your specific gift by activating it**
6. **Work in unity with others whose gifts differ, and win in power of the Holy Spirit**
7. **Gifts are given for God's glory and our victory**

In verse 14, we are encouraged to remember this story and rehearse this message of unity if we want to conquer the enemy in our lives. Moses built an altar and named it, "Jehovah-Nissi," to celebrate the defeat of the Amalekites at Rephidim. Jehovah-Nissi means, "The Lord is My Banner." Let us wave the banner of unity within the church and experience great victory in the world.

~WALK IN UNITY~

Leviticus 17
Power in the Blood

Leviticus 17:11 declares life is in the blood. The driving force of all physical life is blood. Blood is used to fight disease and preserve the quality of our lives. The source of everlasting life is in the blood of Christ.

> *"For this is my blood of the new testament, which is shed for many for the remission of sins."* Matthew 26:28

> *"Wherefore Jesus also, that he might sanctify the people with his own blood, suffered without the gate."* Hebrews 13:12

That makes Jesus the greatest blood donor to ever live. He willingly and sacrificially gave His own blood, so we who are guilty of sin and deserving of a devil's hell can experience eternal life. That is why we, the people of God, can never leave the importance of the Blood of Jesus out of any gospel message we present to the world.

Facts Concerning the Importance of the Blood of Jesus

1. **The Blood of Jesus was shed for the remission of our sins**
   "In whom we have redemption through his blood, the forgiveness of sins, according to the riches of his grace;" Ephesians 1:7

2. **The Blood of Jesus cleanses us from unrighteousness**
   "And from Jesus Christ, who is the faithful witness, and the first begotten of the dead, and the prince of the kings of the earth. Unto him that loved us, and washed us from our sins in his own blood," Revelation 1:5

3. **The Blood of Jesus redeems us**

"In whom we have redemption through his blood, even the forgiveness of sins:" Colossians 1:14

4. The Blood of Jesus gives us peace of God and peace with God

"But now in Christ Jesus ye who sometimes were far off are made nigh by the blood of Christ. For he is our peace, who hath made both one, and hath broken down the middle wall of partition between us;" Ephesians 2:13-14

5. The Blood of Jesus purges our conscience of guilt

"How much more shall the blood of Christ, who through the eternal Spirit offered himself without spot to God, purge your conscience from dead works to serve the living God?" Hebrews 9:14

6. The Blood of Jesus sanctifies us

"And such were some of you: but ye are washed, but ye are sanctified, but ye are justified in the name of the Lord Jesus, and by the Spirit of our God." 1 Corinthians 6:11

7. **The Blood of Jesus releases unity among the church**

   "But now in Christ Jesus ye who sometimes were far off are made nigh by the blood of Christ. For he is our peace, who hath made both one, and hath broken down the middle wall of partition between us;" Ephesians 2:13-14

8. **The Blood of Jesus gives us full access to God**

   "Having therefore, brethren, boldness to enter into the holiest by the blood of Jesus," Hebrews 10:19

9. **The Blood of Jesus is what helps us overcome the devil**

   "And they overcame him by the blood of the Lamb, and by the word of their testimony; and they loved not their lives unto the death." Revelation 12:11

The word "blood" occurs over 440 times in around 350 verses and is the foundation of our Christian faith. If you take blood out of our bodies, we would die; if you take the message of the importance of the Blood of Jesus out of the church, it too will die. The Bible is a dead book without its central message of the Blood of Jesus being emphasized. Never forget the words of the great hymn, "Nothing but the Blood", written by Robert Lowry:

> "What can wash away my sin?
> Nothing but the blood of Jesus;
> What can make me whole again?
> Nothing but the blood of Jesus.
> Oh! precious is the flow
> That makes me white as snow;
> No other fount I know,
> Nothing but the blood of Jesus."

Or the great lyrics from the chorus of "Power in the Blood" written by Lewis E. Jones:

> "There is power, power, wonder-working power
> In the blood of the Lamb.
> There is power, power, wonder-working power
> In the precious blood of the Lamb."

Let's sing about it, talk about it and preach about the precious Blood of the Lamb in 2017.

~POWER IN THE BLOOD OF JESUS~

Numbers 17
Legitimizing Leadership

This is a chapter about how the rod of Aaron miraculously buds to reveal the chosen one of God. Moses and Aaron just dealt with the rebellion of Korah and his followers. Although they witnessed the wrath of God imposed upon those who rebelled against God's chosen leaders, there were still people challenging their authority. Here in Numbers 17, they were questioning Aaron's position as a high priest. So, God creates a test to prove Aaron's God-called position of authority is legitimate. All the leaders of the twelve tribes were to submit a rod, or a branch, with their names written on them. They were to place them before the Ark of the Covenant, and the rod that would produce a bud would indicate the one to be chosen as High Priest. Obviously it was Aaron's rod that budded revealing two qualities that qualified him for the position:

1. **It was alive**
2. **It was fruitful**

Aaron was from the tribe of Levi which, if you remember from Genesis, was considered one of Jacobs's worse sons, Genesis 49:5-7. That passage would clearly suggest any Levites would be at the bottom of the list to be chosen as High Priest. The definition of Levi probably gives us clues as to why he was chosen by God even though he was rejected by man. Levi means, "To be connected and joined together permanently". God, in choosing Aaron, was saying He wanted someone connected to Him to serve in such an important capacity. We should never follow Christian leaders who are not connected to Christ. Leadership should never be chosen by ability or popularity but by someone's closeness to Christ.

> *"If ye abide in me, and my words abide in you, ye shall ask what ye will, and it shall be done unto you. Herein is my Father glorified, that ye bear much fruit; so shall ye be my disciples."* John 15:7-8

The twelve rods initially laid before the Ark were nothing more than dead wood. God's resurrection power brought life into Aaron's rod to reveal who the true leader should be. Just as the resurrection power came into that rod to bring life and reveal the truth, the resurrection of Christ reveals Jesus as the true Messiah. Notice that the rod didn't just come to life and bud, but it also produced fruit. Verse 8, says almonds were actually coming forth. Not only did the rod come to life, but a manifestation of its being alive was that it produced fruit. In other words, it produced something that could be given away and was worth consuming. Some want to lead because they desire a title or want to feel powerful in some way. We are qualified for godly leadership when we are full of life and have something of value to give away. Unless we minister to God first, we will never be able to effectively minister to man. Unless we minister out of an overflow of the Holy Spirit that has been personally activated in us, we can never make a difference in the lives of others. God is legitimizing His true leaders. Don't tolerate the illegitimate in your Christian walk. Look at the Spirit of a man, not the personality of a man.

9 Ways to Identify Legitimate Godly Leaders

1. **Their connection to Christ produces visible life**
2. **They are humble and not jockeying for position**
3. **Their relationship with God matters more than power from God**
4. **They know how to follow others and be faithful**
5. **They know their gifts will ultimately make room for them**
6. **They don't run from but embrace challenges**

7. They are not afraid of a test to prove the godly from the ungodly
8. They have something to give that can be worthily eaten by others
9. They are more interested in the approval of God than the applause of man

~FOLLOW ONLY LEGITIMATE GOD-SENT LEADERS~

Deuteronomy 17
Principled Living

Deuteronomy contains some of the final words of Moses. Here in chapter 17, Moses is touching on 4 main themes that are important for him to establish in the Law. These are timeless principles that help us to be in right standing with God and allow us to position ourselves on the path of success. A principle is, "a moral rule or code of conduct". Principles are beliefs we are devoted to habitually practice in our lives.

4 Principles to Live By

1. **When making an offering to God, give your best,** v. 1
   God gave His best, and we should give our best.

2. **Hold everyone accountable for bad behavior and sin,** v. 2-7

   It's important to take personal responsibility and never place blame or make excuses.

3. **Let all judgments be made using God's Word as our guide,** v. 8-13

   The only way to correctly judge is by using the Word of God.

4. **Always raise the standard of righteousness by walking in integrity,** v. 14-20

   True prophets raise the standard, while false prophets lower the standard. Leaders should always be held to a higher standard of integrity.

These are such awesome truths that we are encouraged to make application of in our lives. We would be well-served to heed the words of Moses, and make them personal laws we live by every single day.

~LIVE A PRINCIPLED LIFE~

Joshua 17
Stop Complaining

There is a lot going on in Joshua 17, but the main topic revolves around people complaining because they don't like the way Joshua is dividing the land. Joshua is listening to their complaints, but Joshua is not petting their devils. He gives them some basic suggestions:

1. **Be thankful for your inheritance**
2. **Don't compare what you have with what others received**
3. **Work to make the land you received better than when you first inherited it**
4. **Don't wait for handouts, go fight if you want more**
5. **Stop complaining, and be content**

We are all responsible to possess the land the Lord has given to us. We must drive out the previous tenants, and stake our claim. Don't compare or compete. Be thankful for what you have received and if you want more, do what needs to be done on your part to make it happen. Let's not find things to complain about in 2017. Make a list from A-Z of things you're thankful for, and start being more appreciative of what God has already given.

A= _____
B= _____
C= _____
D= _____
E= _____
F= _____
G= _____
H= _____
I= _____
J= _____
K= _____
L= _____
M= _____
N= _____
O= _____
P= _____
Q= _____
R= _____
S= _____
T= _____
U= _____
V= _____
W= _____
X= _____
Y= _____
Z= _____

~STOP COMPLAINING~

Judges 17
Discipline Your Children

In these days there was no king, and total anarchy was happening. All kinds of confusion and wild behavior were going on among the people in the country. There were no rules and no laws to govern society. Lawlessness and political disorder were happening because there was an absence of governmental authority. The lack of restraint and disorder was seen here in Judges when a man, by the name of Micah, stole a lot of money from his mother. He later decided to give the money back to his mom, and she was so happy she used some of the stolen silver to make a graven image for him to wear. She rewarded his disobedience instead of bringing correction.

The Bible says in verse 6, that every man did what was right in his own eyes because there was no king or authority. If there is no discipline in the homes, and if there is no parental authority, then we will raise a bunch of thieves and convicts. That may sound harsh, but we have a daddy problem in America. Most of the people in prison have never had a role model, so they learn to survive from people who are rebellious and are not under any authority. Here are some great parental rules, from the Bible, that ought to govern our lives when disciplining our children:

Parental Rules Concerning Discipline

1. Discipline is good for every child
"If ye endure chastening, God dealeth with you as with sons; for what son is he whom the father chasteneth not?" Hebrews 12:7

2. Discipline proves your love for your children
"He that spareth his rod hateth his son: but he that loveth him chasteneth him betimes." Proverbs 13:24

3. Discipline postponed is ineffective
"Chasten thy son while there is hope," Proverbs 19:18a

4. Discipline helps purge wrong conduct from a child
"Foolishness is bound in the heart of a child; but the rod of correction shall drive it far from him." Proverbs 22:15

5. Discipline properly administered won't negatively affect a child

"Withhold not correction from the child: for if thou beatest him with the rod, he shall not die." Proverbs 23:13

6. **Discipline proceeds in spite of crying or resistance**

   "...and let not thy soul spare for his crying." Proverbs 19:18b

7. **Discipline provides help for the child not a release of anger for the adult**

   "And, ye fathers, provoke not your children to wrath: but bring them up in the nurture and admonition of the Lord." Ephesians 6:4

8. **Discipline properly administered now, prepares them for Salvation later**

   "Thou shalt beat him with the rod, and shalt deliver his soul from hell." Proverbs 23:14

This chapter ends with good news when God sends a young godly priest to live with this family. Micah and his mom took this priest in and fed him, clothed him, and gave him a salary. Hope sprung up within Micah, not when he wasn't disciplined but, when he was corrected and given some rules to follow.

"Then said Micah, Now know I that the Lord will do me good, seeing I have a Levite to my priest." Judges 17:13

You might be amazed when you start laying down the law and establishing some rules, how the chaos will end and the blessing will flow.

~EMBRACE CORRECTION AND BE BLESSED~

1 Samuel 17
Slay Your Giants

One of the most famous Bible stories of all time is found within this wonderful chapter of 1 Samuel. It's the story of David and Goliath. David was young and overlooked by his own family, yet God choose him to conquer a giant and lead Israel to supernatural freedom. This chapter gives us the tools to slay our giants and fulfill our destiny.

5 Truths to Fulfilling Our Destiny

1. **Whatever I tolerate, will not change,** v. 23-24

    Tolerating situations and sin only gives them permission to continue.

2. **Understand greatness forces smallness to react,** v. 25-28

   Your call and destiny might anger and aggravate people. Your passion for God and your pursuit of your destiny may make others feel uncomfortable. Usually when people are jealous or miserable in your presence, they find a way to attack you. David's father, brother, and enemy attacked him, but David didn't allow the attack to hinder his destiny.

3. **Logic and Faith are destined to collide,** v. 32-33

   Logic produces facts; faith produces miracles. Never consult logic to determine your destiny.

4. **Your destiny is revealed in steps, not leaps,** v. 34-37

   God imparts information in words and sentences, not in paragraphs or chapters. One encounter with God will not reveal your entire life's work because God is interested in relationships, not events.

5. Resources find people of destiny, v. 40
> My will, my bill
> God's will, God's bill
> Where God guides, He is obligated to provide.

These five truths found in this famous Sunday school story are key to our success in 2017. Use these tools to slay your giants and fulfill your destiny!

~BE A GIANT-SLAYER~

2 Samuel 17
Beware of a Spirit of Ahithophel

The Spirit of Ahithophel can be simply defined as, "unforgiveness". Ahithophel was an extremely wise person. Even David considered Ahithophel's advice to be like getting counsel from God, 2 Samuel 16:23. We read in 1 Chronicles 27:33, that Ahithophel was the king's counselor.

As wise as Ahithotphel was, he entered into some ungodly partnerships and allowed anger and unforgiveness to rule his heart. 2 Samuel 15 tells us of the rebellion against David that was led by his own son Absalom. Absalom was undermining

David's authority for four years by kissing up to people and building relationships with others for his own personal advantage. As the days got closer for Absalom to actually overthrow his father from his kingly position, Absalom called Ahithophel to have a meeting. Remember, Ahithophel was a trusted advisor, even a cabinet member in the kingdom. Here, Absalom is reaching right into the heart of David's inner circle and attempting to have him join the rebellion. The Bible tells us that Ahithophel joined Absalom, and the conspiracy grew even stronger. Others began to think that if this wise man, Ahithophel, had joined Absalom in this massive governmental overthrow, there had to be something going on with David that they didn't know because even his closest confidants were now abandoning him and joining forces with Absalom. So, the question must be asked, "Why would this long time, trusted advisor turn on David and join forces with the enemy?" The answer is simple…unforgiveness.

Ahithophel had a son by the name of Eliam who was actually one of David's mighty men in 2 Samuel 23:34. Eliam had a daughter by the name of Bathsheba which also made her Ahithophel's granddaughter. In 2 Samuel 11, David saw this beautiful woman and inquired about her. David knew who she was and that she was married, but his lustful desires got the best of him; and, not only did he have sex with her, but Bathsheba became pregnant. In David's deep desire to hide his sin and be with Bathsheba, he also killed her husband, Uriah. Then, as you may recall in 2 Samuel 12, the judgment of God fell upon David when the son that was conceived between David and Bathsheba in their unholy union became ill and died. So, Ahithophel had his married granddaughter taken and her husband killed by David. He also lost a great grandson all because of David's inability to control his own fleshly desires. Ahithophel obviously quietly dealt with all these issues, while he faithfully served David, but there was still an underlying thread of unforgiveness that never got resolved. Absalom tapped into that unforgiveness and got Ahithophel to join forces with him.

It's very important to get healed of things instead of just dealing with things because sooner or later, it will surface to lead us astray. Forgiveness is essential to your spiritual health and advancement in 2017. Forgiveness is letting go of your desire for justice and offering grace to someone who has deeply offended you. It's not just important to know what forgiveness is, it's also important to know what forgiveness isn't.

Truths about Forgiveness

- If I forgive, I'm not saying what happened that hurt me is "okay".
- Forgiveness is for me, not just for the offender.
- Forgiveness takes strength. You're not a weak fool to forgive.
- Forgiveness doesn't give the offender permission to hurt me again.
- Forgiveness often takes place when it's painful, not when all the hurt goes away.
- Forgiveness is an act of faith, not feeling.
- Forgiveness doesn't mean a restored relationship.

The Spirit of Ahitophel is alive and well; unforgiveness is running rampant and will destroy everything and everyone in its path. Walk in forgiveness in 2017.

~DON'T BE A GRUDGE-CARRIER~

CHAPTER VI

OLD TESTAMENT SPEAK TO ME – PART 2

1 Kings 17
Recognize True Prophets

Elijah was one of only four people in the Bible who was called "man of God." (1 Kings 17:18) The other three were: Moses in Deuteronomy 33:1, Samuel in 1 Samuel 9:6, and David in Nehemiah 12:24. Elijah faced great highs in ministry and severe lows in life. He was the people's prophet who followed God and experienced some awesome miracles. He was bold and confident in the Lord. Here, in 1 Kings 17, we read of another great Bible story. Let's look at it in five interesting parts:

1. **We are introduced to perhaps the greatest prophet of the Bible,** v. 1a

   Elijah was a bold prophet, and his name means, "wonder-worker". He operated in the Northern Kingdom. Israel was his territory mostly during the reign of Ahab who was an evil king. Ahab was married to Jezebel who became one of Elijah's greatest enemies.

2. **His introduction to the world begins with a prophetic declaration against evil,** v. 1a
Elijah declares to the king that the drought of 3 ½ years won't end until he says it ends.

3. **He goes to the Brook Cherith in obedience to God and is fed by ravens,** v. 2-7
It's obvious from the beginning that when God speaks, Elijah obeys quickly. His obedience brings about blessings that God makes the devil pay for. Ravens are dirty birds that represent evil, but God used them to deliver fresh food every morning and evening.

4. **His divine encounter with a single mom who was a widow,** v. 8-16
When the brook dried up, the word of the Lord came to tell him to go to Zarepath. Again without hesitation, Elijah obeys and meets a single woman with a child whose husband had died. Elijah asked for some food and drink but the woman responds, in verse 12, by telling him she has only enough

for one last meal for herself and her son. She says, "We are going to eat and then starve to death." This was an encounter that was about to yield a miracle as her faith was about to be stretched. Elijah told her to make the last meal for him, and they all would live. She obeyed the prophet and received a prophet's reward.

> *"He that receiveth a prophet in the name of a prophet shall receive a prophet's reward; and he that receiveth a righteous man in the name of a righteous man shall receive a righteous man's reward."* Matthew 10:41

5. The resurrection of her dead child, v. 17-24

You ever feel like you don't even catch your breath from one situation before more drama arises? Well, this is exactly what this widow from Zarapeth is feeling. She obeys the prophet and experiences a miracle, but starting in verse 17, we read of her son who fell sick and died. Thank God the prophet was around. God directs our steps and leads us into blessing when we willingly obey. Initially the single mother got mad at Elijah thinking her son's death was some sort of judgment being imposed as a result of past sin. The prophet quickly calms her and takes the dead boy. He stretches himself out over the boy and prays a 35 word prayer, and life comes back into her son. Everyone won because the prophet obeyed God, and the woman obeyed the prophet.

When a true prophet speaks, it's as good as God saying it because God is using them as His mouthpiece. Learn to recognize the true prophets by judging them and their fruits according to the Word of God.

~RECOGNIZE, RESPOND, AND REWARD THE TRUE PROPHETS OF GOD~

2 Kings 17
Know God

2 Kings describes the downfall of both the Northern Kingdom (Israel) and the Southern Kingdom (Judah). More than one prophet of God warned of impending judgment that would come if they refused the warnings. Israel was destroyed by the Assyrians, and Judah was destroyed by the

Babylonians. This chapter details the depths of despair that Israel, the Northern Kingdom, had fallen into. But as always, God's love and grace enters the situation, and He provides an opportunity for healing by raising up Elijah and Elisha.

There are some great lessons to learn from these wonderful scriptures that reveal the character of God:

Truths Concerning the Nature of God

1. **God hates sin**
   "These six things doth the LORD hate: yea, seven are an abomination unto him: A proud look, a lying tongue, and hands that shed innocent blood, An heart that deviseth wicked imaginations, feet that be swift in running to mischief, A false witness that speaketh lies, and he that soweth discord among brethren." Proverbs 6:16-19

2. **The Lord always judges disobedience**
   "For the wages of sin is death; but the gift of God is eternal life through Jesus Christ our Lord." Romans 6:23

3. **The Lord causes words from true prophets to always come to pass**
   "When a prophet speaketh in the name of the Lord, if the thing follow not, nor come to pass, that is the thing which the Lord hath not spoken, but the prophet hath spoken it presumptuously: thou shalt not be afraid of him." Deuteronomy 18:22

4. **The Lord is faithful**
   "But thou, O Lord, art a God full of compassion, and gracious, long suffering, and plenteous in mercy and truth." Psalm 86:15

5. **The Lord blesses obedience**
   "Ye shall walk in all the ways which the Lord your God hath commanded you, that ye may live, and that it may be well with you, and that ye may prolong your days in the land which ye shall possess." Deuteronomy 5:33

These scriptures help us to know God and how He operates concerning His people. The more you know God, the more you can avoid pitfalls, and have peace in the middle of a storm.

~UNDERSTAND THE NATURE OF GOD~

1 Chronicles 17
Claim the Word

This chapter begins with David feeling a little guilty because he is living in a beautiful, expensive home, while the Ark of the Covenant is a tent where God is living. David somehow speaks or suggests to Nathan that he wants to build a better house for the Ark of the Covenant, and Nathan responds with the famous words from verse 2, *"Do all that is in thine heart; for God is with thee."* God was looking for a permanent building to replace the tent, but David was too consumed with his own personal desires that he couldn't hear from God. God told Nathan to tell David that He didn't want another house. He also told Nathan to relay the message that it would be David's son that would build a new temple. He also declares He is establishing a dynasty for David that would be an enduring legacy even after his death. In verses 16-22, David responds in humility with thanksgiving. Then in verses 23-27, David claims the Word of the Lord. He claims the promise of God. This is a year we must do the same, and claim every promise of God.

> *"Put me in remembrance: let us plead together: declare thou, that thou mayest be justified."* Isaiah 43:26

"(As it is written, I have made thee a father of many nations,) before him whom he believed, even God, who quickeneth the dead, and calleth those things which be not as though they were." Romans 4:17

"And all things, whatsoever ye shall ask in prayer, believing, ye shall receive." Matthew 21:22

"So shall my word be that goeth forth out of my mouth: it shall not return unto me void, but it shall accomplish that which I please, and it shall prosper in the thing whereto I sent it." Isaiah 55:11

"For verily I say unto you, That whosoever shall say unto this mountain, Be thou removed, and be thou cast into the sea; and shall not doubt in his heart, but shall believe that those things which he saith shall come to pass; he shall have whatsoever he saith." Mark 11:23

Use these scriptures in 2017 to help lay hold of all the promises of God.

~CLAIM YOUR PROMISE~

2 Chronicles 17
Godly Leadership

After the death of King Solomon, Israel was divided into two kingdoms. Israel was the Northern Kingdom, and Judah was the Southern Kingdom. Israel had 19 kings, and every one of them were evil. Judah had 20 kings of which 12 were evil, and eight were good. One of the good kings of Judah was the one we read of here in 2 Chronicles 17 by the name of Jehosophat. Jehosophat is the main character for four chapters, and it culminates with the great victory God gave all of Judah in 2 Chronicles 20. God used Jehosophat to bring great revival to Judah and helped turn the people back to God. I am praying for Jehosophat leadership to return to the pulpits of America to help turn our nation back to God and lead us into revival.

Characteristics of Jehosophat Kind of Leadership

1. **He strengthened himself,** v. 1

   The word strengthened, in verse 1, means, "to be intentional about increasing one's value". Godly leadership is always focused on improvement.

2. **He guarded every gate,** v. 2
   Gates are points of entry. Both good and bad have the potential to enter. The gates of the city were guarded to protect the citizens. The gates of our ears, eyes, mouth, and mind should be guarded to protect us against evil invasions.

3. **He had the right mentors,** v. 3a
   He followed the ways of David. He respected the right people and embraced the ideas that made them successful. A mentor is someone who gives worthwhile advice and guidance to less experienced people. Be careful whose advice you follow.

4. **He sought God, not Baal,** v. 3b-4a
   Jehosophat had a heart for God and despised the values of the false god, Baal.

5. **He followed the commandments of God,** v. 4b
   The law of God was important to Jehosophat. He never allowed the ungodly kings from the Northern Kingdom to negatively influence his behavior.

6. **He destroyed everything that didn't glorify God,** v.6

   Let's look through our houses for anything that doesn't please God, and be committed to getting rid of them.

7. **He equipped his leaders,** v. 7

   God doesn't call the equipped, He equips the called.

8. **He walked in unity with those under his authority,** v. 12-15

   God gave rest to them because of their decision to walk in agreement.

Two Main Results of Jehosophat's Godly Leadership

1. Judah experienced a time of peace, v. 10
2. Judah experienced a time of plenty, v. 11-12

Judah was strengthened materially and militarily as a result of Godly leadership. As this sort of leadership begins to be exemplified from the church, the impact will reach beyond the walls of our churches and into our communities.

~LEAD GODLY IN 2017~

Job 17
Finish Strong

This chapter reveals Job's lowest emotional point, where in his weakness he shares his true feelings. He said in the very first verse,

1. My spirit is broken
2. My days are used up
3. My grave is ready

It's clear he feels at the end of his rope and has little hope. The troubles have worn him out, and he is ready to die. Not only has he lost everything, but his mockers, or "friends", are staring and mocking at him. He tried to help them help him in the previous chapter, but his advice fell on deaf ears.

Then something happens...he turns to God in verse 3:

> *"Lay down now, put me in a surety with thee; who is he that will strike hands with me?"*

He calls out to God and makes a deal with the Lord that was sealed with a handshake. Job wants assurance that God is on his side and that his so called friends would be more understanding. He continues, in verses 6-10, to plead his cause to those who have added salt to the wound. With his physical and emotional condition deteriorating, he is still trying to convince others that he is not a hypocrite. He doesn't want people to think he did something wrong to deserve this horrible judgment. He is speaking, but no one is listening. He has allowed his misfortunes to change his plans. In verse 11, his personal feelings are growing dimmer as he says,

1. My days are past
2. I have no purpose
3. My thoughts aren't even valuable

Then Job asks 4 questions:

1. Where is my hope?
2. Who can see my hope?
3. Will my hope go with me to the grave?
4. Shall I and my hope rest in the ground?

I wish this chapter ended with more optimism, but some chapters in our lives don't always have a happy ending. Maybe you are going through some things, and some chapters of your life are ending in discouragement. The book doesn't have to be finished. There can be more chapters left to be written. It doesn't matter how you start, it matters how you finish. Between the cradle and the crown there is a cross to bear.

> *"Wherefore seeing we also are compassed about with so great a cloud of witnesses, let us lay aside every weight, and the sin which doth so easily beset us, and let us run with patience the race that is set before us, Looking unto Jesus the author and finisher of our faith; who for the joy that was set before him endured the cross, despising the shame, and is set down at the right hand of the throne of God."* Hebrews 12:1-2

Don't allow discouragement to get the best of you. Let God rewrite your story, and never give up because there is more to your story.

~BE A FINISHER~

Psalm 17
Divine Disappointments

Disappointment is usually used in a negative sense; however, when used in reference to the enemy, it can be positive. This Psalm is a prayer of David that comes in a moment of true concern for this man of God. His faith was not at its highest point, and he is dealing with discouragement. Nothing seems to be going his way, and he declares in verse 12 that his enemy is greedy and lurking in secret places waiting to pounce on him and destroy him. He musters up enough courage to say, "Disappoint the enemy." Let the enemy fail to fulfill his expectations concerning me. Rob my enemy of its hopes and desires. Upset his plan, and intervene to divinely disappoint the enemy. We need to always remind ourselves that everyone will not be excited about our service to God. Just as Jesus had enemies, we also will have enemies. Enemies are a sign you're doing something right, or the devil wouldn't fight you so much. Your enemies are actually more essential to your destiny being fulfilled than your supporters can be. Friends comfort, but enemies can bring promotion. David's promotion to king came as Goliath rose up against Israel, and he was willing to take up the fight. When you feel like you're losing ground, and the enemy is waiting in the bushes to jump out and destroy, began to remember these scriptures:

> *"And let us not be weary in well doing: for in due season we shall reap, if we faint not."*
> Galatians 6:9

"No weapon that is formed against thee shall prosper; and every tongue that shall rise against thee in judgment thou shalt condemn. This is the heritage of the servants of the Lord, and their righteousness is of me, saith the Lord." Isaiah 54:17

"How God anointed Jesus of Nazareth with the Holy Ghost and with power: who went about doing good, and healing all that were oppressed of the devil; for God was with him." Acts 10:38

"And having spoiled principalities and powers, he made a shew of them openly, triumphing over them in it." Colossians 2:15

"For I am persuaded, that neither death, nor life, nor angels, nor principalities, nor powers, nor things present, nor things to come, Nor height, nor depth, nor any other creature, shall be able to separate us from the love of God, which is in Christ Jesus our Lord." Romans 8:38-39

"And they overcame him by the blood of the Lamb, and by the word of their testimony; and they loved not their lives unto the death." Revelation 12:11

> *"He that committeth sin is of the devil; for the devil sinneth from the beginning. For this purpose the Son of God was manifested, that he might destroy the works of the devil."* 1 John 3:8

Always remember the resurrection of Jesus Christ was the greatest divine disappointment the devil has ever had. Romans 8:11 says that same spirit lives in us. So, don't be defeated; there are more divine disappointments headed in the direction of the devil.

~MAKE AN APPOINTMENT TO DISAPPOINTMENT THE ENEMY~

Proverbs 17
Godly Resolutions

If you are looking to develop some godly new year's resolutions, this is a perfect Proverb to look at. I call Proverbs 17 the "New Year's Resolution Proverb". All the Proverbs are full of truth and wisdom, so it's smart to pay attention, and make application of these principles every day to achieve great success on a yearly basis:

1. Walk in unity with everyone, v. 1

2. Seek the wisdom of God, v. 2
3. Be faithful when tested, v. 3
4. Watch your tongue, v. 4
5. Help the poor and unfortunate, v. 5
6. Leave a legacy for and deposit good into young people, v. 6
7. Never lie, v. 7
8. Don't spend more than you make, v. 8
9. Be discreet and modest in your behavior, v. 9
10. Embrace correction, v. 10
11. Avoid rebellion, v. 11
12. Control your passion, v. 12
13. Don't reward evil, v. 13
14. Never interfere in others concerns unless first invited to offer assistance, v. 14
15. Love what God loves; hate what God hates, v. 15
16. Put your heart into everything you do, v. 16
17. Be a true friend, v. 17
18. Study the Word for understanding, v. 18
19. End arguments quickly, v. 19

20. Don't provoke others to evil, v. 20

21. Fulfill all parental responsibility, v. 21

22. Laugh more, v. 22

23. Don't be for sale to the highest bidder, v. 23

24. Stay focused, v. 24

25. Make someone's day, every day, v.25

26. Treat followers with kindness, v. 26

27. Seek excellence, not perfection, v. 27

28. Listen more, speak less, v. 28

There are plenty of wonderful things to seek after each and every day of the year to positively affect your relationship with God. Some of these are difficult tasks but God will anoint your humble efforts to draw closer to Him.

~SEEK GOD'S WILL IN 2017~

Isaiah 17
Avoid Temptation

The people of Ephraim and Damascus have forgotten God and turned to idols to offer their worship. God is angry and pronouncing His judgment upon them because of their disobedience. Here is a list of their coming judgment:

- Their towns will be destroyed
- Their population will decrease
- They will lose their influence and power
- The glory of God will depart from their presence
- Famine will come to their land
- Anything they plant will die before it can be harvested
- Great physical pain will be imposed upon them
- They will be afraid at night

These are some destructive consequences that are falling upon them because of the continual rebellion. Here are some good scriptures to remind ourselves when the temptation to sin becomes great:

> *"Be not deceived; God is not mocked: for whatsoever a man soweth, that shall he also reap. For he that soweth to his flesh shall of the flesh reap corruption; but he that soweth to the Spirit shall of the Spirit reap life everlasting."* Galatians 6:7-8

"The Lord is not slack concerning his promise, as some men count slackness; but is longsuffering to us-ward, not willing that any should perish, but that all should come to repentance." 2 Peter 3:9

"The heart is deceitful above all things, and desperately wicked: who can know it? I the Lord search the heart, I try the reins, even to give every man according to his ways, and according to the fruit of his doings." Jeremiah 17:9-10

"For he is the minister of God to thee for good. But if thou do that which is evil, be afraid; for he beareth not the sword in vain: for he is the minister of God, a revenger to execute wrath upon him that doeth evil." Romans 13:4

"But your iniquities have separated between you and your God, and your sins have hid his face from you, that he will not hear." Isaiah 59:2

~AVOID EVERY KIND OF EVIL~

Jeremiah 17
Examine Your Heart

Jeremiah 17 is basically a discourse to God's people on the condition of their hearts. Jeremiah was a man of passion and conviction. He wasn't afraid to speak up and share unpopular ideas that God laid upon his heart. Jeremiah's desire was to please God and then declare His truth. When Jeremiah began to observe the condition of God's people, he discerned there were four different kinds of hearts that could define the condition of the nation.

Four Conditions of the Heart

1. **Divided Hearts,** v. 1-4

   Judah was divided in their devotion. They held on to God with one hand while holding on to Baal with the other. God's anger was being kindled against them because of their double mindedness.

2. **Departed Hearts,** v. 5-6

   The difference between a divided heart and a departed heart is that both hands are holding on to the things of the world. You're not a fence-rider or a pole-sitter, you have totally turned your back on God and have fully engaged yourself in sin. Jeremiah said a departed heart will lose its inheritance. Beware because a little sin can end up spoiling the whole lot.

3. Devoted Hearts, v. 7-8

A devoted heart is a heart that is dedicated to walking in obedience. It's a loving and loyal commitment that doesn't waver. It is a heart that is sold out and feeds itself on the Word of God, so growth can always take place.

4. Deceitful Hearts, v. 9-11

The worst deception is not deceiving others but its deceiving yourself.

> *"For the word of God is quick, and powerful, and sharper than any twoedged sword, piercing even to the dividing asunder of soul and spirit, and of the joints and marrow, and is a discerner of the thoughts and intents of the heart."* Hebrews 4:12

Just as Eve was deceived and led Adam astray, we too sometimes are not fair when it comes to accessing the condition of our hearts. When we walk in deception, we cheat ourselves of the progress we could make if we didn't have a wrong impression of ourselves. Judge your fruit and not your feelings according to the Word to validate your fleshly conclusions.

Make a true assessment of the condition of your heart in 2017. If you're not passing the test, repent, and turn from your evil ways. There is still time to change.

~CHECK THE CONDITION OF YOUR HEART~

Ezekiel 17
Unstoppable Deliverance

The Lord is giving a riddle to the prophet of God to use as a parable to help Israel to solve a problem and understand a truth that they are just not grasping. This chapter reveals the patience of God with His rebellious and ignorant children. This is not His first effort to show His people how they have broken their covenant with God. God is frustrated but continues to make attempts to get beyond their deaf and dumb spirit. The Lord has always called His chosen leaders to a higher level of integrity, and God is upset that there has been a lowering of that standard. Great sin has crept its way into the royalty of the kingdom.

Here are just some of the sins that were tolerated in the land:

- Dishonest transactions
- Witchcraft
- Idol worship
- Murder
- No boundaries
- Lying
- Bribery
- Church was corrupt
- Breaking of oaths
- Searing of conscience

Ezekiel was God's prophetic man for this dark hour who would reveal to God's people His message. Ezekiel was a Jew that lived in Babylon about 500 miles from his home in Judah. He was a prisoner in captivity about 600 years before the birth of Jesus. Ezekiel was in prison when the Babylonians took some of Judah's most important people into captivity. In verse 3, God is comparing the taking of Judah's King Jehoiachin, who was related to David, to an eagle breaking off the top of a cedar and planting it in another country. After taking King Jehoiachin, the Babylonians installed Zedekiah as King. Zedekiah was also a descendant of David but was not necessarily a godly king. Zedekiah should have ruled under the authority for the Babylonians but rebelled and attempted to join with the Egyptians to destroy the Babylonians. 2 Kings 25:6-7 tells us that Zedekiah's rebellion was found out, and he had his eyes gouged out before taken to Babylon and put in prison. David's dynasty had, in the natural, appeared to have come to an end. God was making a vow to Ezekiel and His people that no matter how it looked in the natural, God Himself would raise up a descendant from the house of David, as prophesied in the Old Testament, to cultivate that top of cedar wood that was planted in a new land to bring deliverance to His people. Jesus is that seed!! Jesus descended from David through the virgin Mary. Ezekiel 17 is really a prophetic word released to encourage those bound in a foreign land that the plan of God cannot be stopped. God was mad that it appeared all hope was lost, and His people bought into the lies of the enemy.

> *"No weapon that is formed against thee shall prosper; and every tongue that shall rise against thee in judgment thou shalt condemn. This is the heritage of the servants*

of the Lord, and their righteousness is of me, saith the Lord." Isaiah 54:17

No matter what you go through in 2017 or how it may appear, always remind yourself God's deliverance is unstoppable.

~GOD WILL DELIVER~

CHAPTER VII

NEW TESTAMENT SPEAK TO ME

Matthew 17
The Glory of the Lord

In Matthew 17, we read of the transfiguration of Christ. The word, "transfiguration", signifies a change of the appearance. In Luke 9:27, Jesus says, *"But I tell you of a truth, there be some standing here, which shall not taste of death, till they see the kingdom of God."*

Matthew 17 is a prophetic fulfillment of Luke 9:27. Jesus' inner circle is getting a glimpse of things to come. Jesus took them up a mountain to pray to strengthen their faith before the coming crucifixion. He transfigured, or changed, in front of them as He revealed His glory. His face shined as the sun, and He was clothed in white. It was intended to be an encouragement to them, no matter what was about to happen that everything was going to be alright. Moses and Elijah appeared as the two principal parts of the Old Testament that represented the Law and the prophets. Moses was the giver of the Law, and Elijah was considered the greatest of the prophets. It was a sign to Peter,

James, and John that the coming death and resurrection of Christ was connected to Old Testament heritage.

> *"Think not that I am come to destroy the law, or the prophets: I am not come to destroy, but to fulfil."* Matthew 5:17

Jesus didn't come to destroy the Law but to fulfill It. The transfiguration was a temporary manifestation that released momentary joy. Sometimes God gives us visions, or glimpses, of His glory to comfort us from the past or encourage us from what is to come.

After this awesome revealing of His glory, the other disciples, who weren't a part of the transfiguration, met a man who had a son that was possessed. The disciples were powerless in their efforts to deliver him. When the father mentioned this to Jesus, the Lord was frustrated and verbally corrected them for their lack of discernment and faith. Immediately Jesus rebuked the devil, and the son was delivered. When the disciples asked why they couldn't cast the devil out, Jesus responded because of their unbelief and inability to understand that sometimes you must add fasting to your prayer. This was a situation they were unprepared to handle. When it comes to God revealing or releasing His glory, as in Matthew 17, God always wants us to be prepared and ready for what is to happen. Get ready for God to reveal His glory to sustain you in future trials and release His glory through you to demonstrate His power to others.

~REVEALING & RELEASING THE GLORY OF THE LORD~

Luke 17
Forgiveness, Thanks*living*, and the Coming of the Lord

When you take the whole chapter in context there are three main subjects to focus on in 2017:

1. **Forgiveness,** v. 1-10
2. **Thanks*living*,** v. 11-19
3. **Return of Christ,** v. 20-37

Forgiveness

When it comes to forgiveness, it's important to remember, it doesn't matter WHO is right as much as WHAT is right. Jesus warned that all of us will be offended and the potential for unforgiveness to reside in our hearts is probable. We are taught to forgive others even if it is a repeated offense. We can't control others and what they do, but we can control our response. We can't allow a bad response of unforgiveness to affect our witness to others. It's clear the disciples also connected faith with forgiveness. They asked the Lord to increase their faith after Jesus spoke on the need to forgive. It isn't easy to forgive others who intentionally hurt us. What we can't do naturally, we must ask for faith to do supernaturally.

Thanks*living*

Notice the word, "Thanks*living*". It's living a life where you are thankful. Luke 17:11-19 records one of the saddest stories of unthankfulness. Ten lepers were healed, but only one gave thanks. Leprosy is mostly a Biblical disease, but its negative symptoms went beyond the contagious bacterial infection. It caused painful nerve damage, muscle weakness, and open sores. Leprosy also affected people emotionally because they were isolated, quarantined, and personally rejected. To be healed of such a horrible disease, ought to have brought words of thanks from everyone. Sometimes it's not always a sense of entitlement or unthankfulness that stops us from expressing thanksgiving, but it's getting caught up in the moment and not remembering we should be grateful. If we live a life of thanks*living* it's easier to take the time to express it. Let's live thanks and not just give thanks.

Return of Christ

Jesus was being questioned by the Pharisees as to when the Kingdom of God was coming. They weren't sincerely seeking an answer. They were trying to get him to make statements that they could use against Him. Jesus said although there is a day of the coming of the Lord, the Kingdom of God is already within you. He also laid out several signs to watch for that would reveal the coming of the Lord would be soon:

1. **A lack of spiritual awareness,** v. 20
2. **Great suffering,** v. 25a
3. **Rejection of godly things,** v. 25
4. **Spiritual ignorance that is unparalleled since the days of Noah and Lot,** v. 25-30
5. **Backsliding will be unprecedented,** v. 31-32
6. **Selfishness will abound,** v. 33a
7. **Lack of discernment,** v. 34-36

Let's make sure, as the coming of the Lord nears, that we walk in forgiveness, and live a life of gratitude. These are two very important traits that will internally prepare us for the Lord's return.

~COME QUICKLY~

John 17
Power of Prayer

This chapter is totally the words of Jesus as He offers His final words of instruction to His disciples about prayer. This is the largest recorded prayer of Jesus, and it revolves around three main parts:

1. **Prayer for Himself,** v. 1-8
2. **Prayer for His Disciples,** v. 9-19
3. **Prayer for the Church,** v. 20-26

Prayer for Himself

Jesus understands that His time on earth is coming to an end, and the sacrifice of the Cross is getting closer. Jesus is acknowledging that He has completed the job He was sent to do by the Father. There is a sense of relief and yet frustration in that the people didn't fully receive Him. Maybe He even felt unappreciated by those who rejected His efforts of love. We need to be reminded that Jesus could only help those who wanted to help themselves. When we have done our best and given everything to the Lord, let's learn how to leave the results up to God. Let's also pray for a refreshing to come to us as we connect with the Father as Jesus did here in this chapter.

Prayer for His Disciples

He was praying for those who had sacrificed their lives to follow Him. There was a sense of appreciation that Jesus was expressing to the Father because of the faithfulness of the disciples. His prayer was five-fold:

1. **He prayed for joy,** v. 13
2. **He prayed for the Word to remain in them to avoid worldly things,** v. 14
3. **He prayed for their continual protection,** v. 15
4. **He prayed for their sanctification,** v. 17
5. **He prayed that they would spread the Good News,** v. 18

These are awesome things to remember in our lives that we should apply on a daily basis.

Prayer for the Church

No less than four times in seven verses, He mentions the importance of oneness in the church. Unity was the last message of Jesus to His church in His final prayer. Our country has never been more divided in my lifetime than it is right now. If we are ever going to have unity, we must learn oneness isn't sameness. We can be different and still be one. Let's pray the prayer of Jesus begins to bring unity in our land. Prayer is more important than ever in 2017. This is an important prayer to study and apply as the coming of the Lord approaches.

~PRAY FOR UNITY~

Acts 17
Advance the Kingdom of God

Paul was called a troublemaker by the leaders in Thessalonica who had heard of what Paul had accomplished for God in other cities. They tried to discredit the people of God to hinder their potential influence.

Three Things we need in order to impact the Kingdom of God

1. **Integrity**

    The people of Acts 17 were looking for something real and authentic. They desired for something more than the Jewish and pagan cultures could offer. The culture was filled with sexual permissiveness and immorality. There were some who were fed up and wanted something different. Paul's sincerity and integrity came across as he spoke in the synagogue and on Mars Hill and preached an uncompromising Word of the Lord. The measure of a man's character is determined by what he would do if no one ever found out. It's like the story of the letter one man wrote to the IRS:

Dear IRS,

I'm not sleeping very well lately because last year I misrepresented my income. So, I am enclosing a check for $500.00.

Ps. If I still can't sleep, I will send in the rest.

Doing the right thing the right way and doing it every time is what integrity is all about.

2. Intensity

Paul was intense in his belief system. He wasn't playing games. He was serious in wanting to fulfill the plans of God. Intense means, "To be extremely enthusiastic". It's a godly passion and fervency that surpasses human emotion. It's being compelled to be committed to serving God and hating evil enough to speak up against it. We need a holy intensity to invade our hearts as Christians. Let's never back down and always stand up for what is godly.

3. Involvement

We have too many backseat drivers and armchair quarterbacks in the church. They don't want to get involved but want to tell everyone else how to do things. Here in Acts 17, the Christians were getting involved in the lives of the Jews and developing relationships, not just using them to gain notoriety, by winning them to Christ. Jason was inviting leaders and others into his own house even though he knew it could cause him trouble. Let's care enough to get involved, and stop making excuses when it comes to reaching out to a lost and dying world.

If the church is going to be successful in this modern age, we must have these three qualities as a part of our lives. We can't compromise and lower our standards if we want to advance the Kingdom of God.

~ADVANCE THE KINGDOM OF GOD~

Revelation 17
Destruction of the Unfaithful

The term "woman" is used as a symbol for the church in 2 Corinthians 11:1-2:

> *"Would to God ye could bear with me a little in my folly: and indeed bear with me. For I am jealous over you with godly jealousy: for I have espoused you to one husband, that I may present you as a chaste virgin to Christ."*

Here the true church is depicted as an engaged woman to her fiancé, Jesus Christ. The woman here in Revelation is considered and called a "harlot" or "great whore". The once faithful woman has entered into adultery with the leaders and concerns of this world. Her behavior has not only infected her, but it has spread to others as she is giving birth to other harlots and engaging in pagan practices. She is seen riding the beast which suggests a relationship between the once true church and the anti-Christ. She is adorned with wealth and has a position of influence. With all the information about her, she is still referred to as a "mystery" in verses 5-7.

What isn't a mystery is the judgment that will ultimately fall upon those who faithfully served the Lord, but for whatever reason have turned their backs on God, joined forces with the Evil One, and make an effort to mislead others away from Christ. Notice in the beginning of chapter 17, she is sitting on the Beast, but at the end of chapter 17, she is being utterly devoured and destroyed.

> *"Yet ye have forsaken me, and served other gods: wherefore I will deliver you no more."* Judges 10:13

> *"And they transgressed against the God of their fathers, and went a whoring after the gods of the people of the land, whom God destroyed before them."* 1 Chronicles 5:25

> *"And I will make the land desolate, because they have committed a trespass, saith the Lord God."* Ezekiel 15:8

> *"Thou hast forsaken me, saith the Lord, thou art gone backward: therefore will I stretch out my hand against thee, and destroy thee; I am weary with repenting."* Jeremiah 15:6

> *"For, lo, they that are far from thee shall perish: thou hast destroyed all them that go a whoring from thee."* Psalm 73:27

> *"Remember, I beseech thee, the word that thou commandedst thy servant Moses,*

saying, If ye transgress, I will scatter you abroad among the nations:" Nehemiah 1:8

Don't fall for the lure and lies of the enemy. Remember, Matthew 24:24,

"For there shall arise false Christs, and false prophets, and shall shew great signs and wonders; insomuch that, if it were possible, they shall deceive the very elect."

Stay connected to the Lord and His Holy Word to avoid deception. Be accountable to authority, and don't reject the correction that can sometimes come to avoid demonic traps. The faithful prosper, the unfaithful will be destroyed.

~STAY FAITHFUL~

Summary of Chapter 17's

Genesis 17 - Rewrite Your Story
Exodus 17 - Working Together: Winning Together
Leviticus 17 - Power in the Blood
Numbers 17 - Legitimizing Leadership
Deuteronomy 17 - Principled Living
Joshua 17 - Stop Complaining
Judges 17 - Discipline Your Children
1 Samuel 17 - Slay Your Giants
2 Samuel 17 - Beware of a Spirit of Ahithophel
1 Kings 17 - Recognize True Prophets
2 Kings 17 - Know God
1 Chronicles 17 - Claim the Word
2 Chronicles 17 - Godly Leadership
Job 17 - Finish Strong
Psalm 17 - Divine Disappointments
Proverbs 17 - Godly Resolutions
Isaiah 17 - Avoid Temptation
Jeremiah 17 - Examine Your Heart
Ezekiel 17 - Unstoppable Deliverance
Matthew 17 - The Glory of the Lord
Luke 17 - Forgiveness, Thanks*living*, & the Coming of the Lord
John 17 - Power of Prayer
Acts 17 - Advance the Kingdom
Revelation 17 - Destruction of the Unfaithful

CHAPTER VIII

SPIRITUAL FORECAST FOR ALL 50 STATES

This is always one portion of the book that everyone seems to love. It's probably because we want to know what God is saying and doing wherever we make the greatest investment of our time. In 2017, the Lord has impressed upon me to tell you to watch the capital cities of each state, specifically the one you live in. I've included them with each prophecy, so when you look back at the specific prophetic words, you can remember to pray for the political center of your state.

The word "capital" in the Latin is "Caput" and means "Head". A capital city is a city of chief importance within a state. It's from the capital cities that policies are developed and passed that influence the rest of the state. Capital cities are usually large in size but are not always the largest city. The capital cities of each state are important to watch in 2017. The revealing light of God will shine in our capital cities and reveal the truth for those who are walking in deceit. Every person should know who their representatives are, and how they vote, so we the people can hold them accountable. I also encourage you to contact those State and US Representatives that represent you, and let them know you are praying for them.

Keep your eyes and ears open for what will be exposed in 2017. We need to prophecy to our states, and it starts with prophesying over our capital cities. Let's believe God to expose corruption and political excess as well as allow a spirit of revival to penetrate the political centers of our states. Please read the prophecy for your particular state, but also as news unfolds throughout the year, look back to see connections with the God-given words that have been released.

Alabama

Scripture: *"Then I said unto them, What is the high place whereunto ye go? And the name whereof is called Bamah unto this day."* Ezekiel 20:29

Book Study: Genesis

> ***Prophetic Word:*** *You are going up to the high places in January 2017, but then be prepared for the heavy rains to fall in the summer. I desire for you to go further, deeper, and higher with Me in your spiritual walk. Don't allow the minor things to be your major focus. Meditate on what's important to Me, and make every effort not to just "hear" the Word but to "do" the Word. You are a key state in the South to allow revival to be released in the region, but you can't go through the motions. Study Joel, and believe for Me to increase your faith.*

Capital: Montgomery
Key Month: January
Pray For: Unity and Faith

Alaska

Scripture: *"The backslider in heart shall be filled with his own ways: and a good man shall be satisfied from himself."* Proverbs 14:14

Book Study: Psalms

> ***Prophetic Word:*** *In 2017, you will begin to reap what you have sown. It's taken a while to manifest, but now is the time for the faithful and the faithless to give account and receive their just reward. For those who have lowered the standard and allowed compromise of My Word to be a reality in your life, don't be upset when the faithful remain standing. You will see favor come to those who have obeyed and applied My truths. You will experience how favor isn't always fair. My favor is released on those who have pursued Me with all their hearts and have made obedience to My Word a priority. Pay close attention to your natural resources being reduced and it being publicized in the national spotlight.*

Capital: Juneau
Key Month: September
Pray for: Obedience to God's Word

Arizona

Scripture: *"Yea, though I walk through the valley of the shadow of death, I will fear no evil: for thou art with me; thy rod and thy staff they comfort me."* Psalm 23:4

Book Study: Nahum

> ***Prophetic Word:*** *I am restarting your engine and refiring your spirit. I am not done with you, so don't relax and sit on your past victories. There is much to do, and although you have been hidden for a time, you're about to rise to the top. Quit reasoning away My requests to step up, and know that I will give you the strength to complete the task, and I will supply every tool to ensure your success. Don't allow timidity to enter the picture. Stand up, and be courageous. Spring is your time of preparation, but fall is your time of prosperity. The earth may shake and split all around you, but I am with you always.*

Capital: Phoenix
Key Month: October
Pray For: Courage

Arkansas

Scripture: *"Truly my soul waiteth upon God: from him cometh my salvation."* Psalm 62:1

Book Study: 2 Corinthians

> ***Prophetic Word:*** *The two shall become one in your state. The divided things will be brought back together. Families, finances, jobs, politics, bodies of water, dry ground, etc. will be restored. Prophesy what you want according to My Word, and you will have it. Call things forth, and don't doubt. This is a critical season for you to seize the righteous things. Don't look back, more forward into your destiny. Protect the rivers in the spring, and release the natural resources that have been given for your prosperity.*

Capital: Little Rock
Key Month: July
Pray For: Restoration

California

Scripture*: "Ask, and it shall be given you; seek, and ye shall find; knock, and it shall be opened unto you: For every one that asketh receiveth; and he that seeketh findeth; and to him that knocketh it shall be opened."* Matthew 7:7-8

Book Study: Galatians

> ***Prophetic Word:*** *Be specific, be persistent, and be expectant in your praying. You have forgotten to ask, and when you have asked, you've missed the mark. Manipulation doesn't control Me, education doesn't influence Me, and desperation doesn't intimidate Me. Faith is the only voice I honor. My people need to take the lead on things that need changed. Combine fasting with your prayer, and document the results. You will need to exhibit God-Faith in 2017, for challenges will arise, and the nation will be sent to help in times of trouble. Don't allow your spirit to be crushed but turn obstacles into opportunities that will allow others to sense My Spirit within you. Be a witness of My goodness.*

Capital: Sacramento
Key Month: March
Pray For: Faith

Colorado

Scripture: *"But if the Spirit of him that raised up Jesus from the dead dwell in you, he that raised up Christ from the dead shall also quicken your mortal bodies by his Spirit that dwelleth in you."* Romans 8:11

Book Study: Nehemiah

> ***Prophetic Word:*** *I am calling you to avoid perfection, and seek excellence in 2017. I desire for you to go beyond the normal and ordinary. You have blended in, but I want you to stand out. Excellence is not a gift and must be earnestly sought after with a heart of humility. Begin to have a greater desire to impress Me instead of just promoting yourself. You have accepted mediocrity as a way of life. You've blamed others, missed deadlines, and have been disorganized, yet you have expected promotion. There is no conspiracy against you. You and your acceptance of the ordinary is what is holding you back. Greatness awaits your effort to put Me first and cultivate what I have already placed inside of you. The winter will be rough in a lot of realms, but pursue excellence, and achieve the extraordinary.*

Capital: Denver
Key Month: February
Pray For: A Hunger for God

Connecticut

Scripture: *"Trust in the Lord with all thine heart; and lean not unto thine own understanding. In all thy ways acknowledge him, and he shall direct thy paths."* Proverbs 3:5-6

Book Study: Mark

> ***Prophetic Word:*** *Your complacency has kept you from growing and has created feelings of incompetence. You have lost your motivation, and self-doubt has replaced your confidence. You have, in many ways, settled in and have become apathetic with things around you. But, your place of comfort is becoming uncomfortable. Never allow your fear of change to outweigh the amazing experiences and life-changing events that I have for you to enjoy. If you will allow Me to enter your life, I will help you find things you never knew existed. Situations from the past, and people in your present, are keeping you from being what I created you to be. You are being held back and trapped in a life that is far from the life I've intended*

you to live. Stop allowing others to block the call that is on your life. Your purpose is found in seeking Me with your whole heart.

Capital: Hartford
Key Month: July
Pray For: Deliverance

Delaware

Scripture: *"Regard not them that have familiar spirits, neither seek after wizards, to be defiled by them: I am the Lord your God."* Leviticus 19:31

Book Study: Philippians

> ***Prophetic Word:** Return to your spiritual roots, and quit dabbling in the evil behavior that is dragging you downward. Your respect for Me has dwindled over time, and there is no longer a respect that causes you to be conscious of the consequences of sin. Your desire to please the flesh and satisfy your own cravings has left distaste in My mouth. I am calling My true bride to rise and curse the darkness. Penetrate the evil with the light of My Word. Pray against witchcraft and other occult behavior. The News will reveal animal and human sacrifices that have occurred, to shed a*

spotlight on the injustice that has gone on because of a lack of the fear of God. You, My bride, rise up, and declare a different way, and see others turn to the Lord.

Capital: Dover
Key Month: August
Pray For: Occult activity to be revealed

Florida

Scripture: *"Be sober, be vigilant; because your adversary the devil, as a roaring lion, walketh about, seeking whom he may devour:"* 1st Peter 5:8

Book Study: John

***Prophetic Word:** Stir up your gift, and arise out of the spirit of slumber that has laid its hold on you. It's time to arouse the gifts, and arise to greatness. Though you're in the lower parts I want to take you to the highest of places. Don't allow the old excuses, or past experiences, to block a new move of My Spirit, that I want to flood this state with in 2017. Tourism is on the rise, and My glory is flowing down. You must stay connected, and trust Me. I will remove every roadblock and obstacle from your view, so you can* *reach your intended destination, but your eyes must be looking upon Me. I desire for you to bring joy to the nation. You are a melting pot of people, so work in unity to achieve success, and walk in My power. Watch the borders in the spring and the waters in the summer.*

Capital: Tallahassee
Key Month: August
Pray For: Energy, Persistence and Discernment

Georgia

Scripture: *"In the beginning was the Word, and the Word was with God, and the Word was God."* John 1:1

Book Study: Colossians

***Prophetic Word:** It is of the upmost importance that you stand on guard with your eyes open and are prepared for battle in 2017. You can't go through the motions or allow your feelings and emotions to rule you any longer. I have a plan for you, but it is incumbent upon you to cooperate with Me. You played a key role last year in bringing about My will, but now is not a time to rest or pout. Your work has just begun, so* *prepare yourself with the armor of God, and use My Word to fight off those attacks that have come to divert you off course. Your mouth is to be used to fight with praise, and your hands are designed to point others in the right direction. I am counting on you, so rise to the task, and fulfill your God-given purpose in this life.*

Capital: Atlanta
Key Month: May
Pray For: Increase in Leadership

Hawaii

Scripture: *"As the hart panteth after the water brooks, so panteth my soul after thee, O God."* Psalm 42:1

Book study: Daniel

> ***Prophetic Word:*** *You are a unique people in many ways, so I am visiting you in 2017. I will be in the fire and in the rain. I will be in the sky and in the earth. I will be with you at all times and in all places. I will be there when you feel Me close and when you think I am far away. If you see only one set of footprints, it's not yours, but it's Me carrying you through the storms of life. I will never*

leave you or forsake you. I love you, and you will experience a new level of love throughout this year. As I show you, you will show others the love that only the LORD can offer to them.

Capital: Honolulu
Key Month: December
Pray For: Open hearts to receive and release the love God

Idaho

Scripture: *"Casting all your care upon him; for he careth for you."* 1 Peter 5:7

Book Study: Luke

***Prophetic Word:** This is a year of prayer for this state. You have carried an unnecessary burden for a prolonged period of time. Prayer will help to empty the cares of your heart that have been weighing you down and holding you back from a full pursuit of Me. Hanna had a promise, but the cares of this life brought her a sorrowful spirit that kept her from receiving the promise of God. She had to go to the altar and unload on God before she could become pregnant. Unload on Me. When you pray, it acknowledges that* *your need is beyond your human ability to solve. You don't have to know the answer; you just have to know who to call. It causes humility to enter your life as you grasp an understanding that if God can't do it, then it can't be done. Prayer will give you divine direction, as Jonah had to learn, when he made a decision without prayer, and it lead to destruction. I want to save you, but prayer is your key. Isaiah said, "God is your wonderful counselor." You have got to stop making decisions without God. Prayer is your umbilical cord between heaven and earth. God's will is already done in heaven, but He needs you to help bring it to pass on earth. Prayer strengthens our relationship with God as we understand it's a dialogue not a monologue. You pray, and I will listen, but be silent, and allow Me to talk while you listen. Prayer will change you and mold you into the image of God.*

Capital: Boise
Key Month: February
Pray For: Talking and listening to God

Illinois

Scripture: *"Therefore if any man be in Christ, he is a new creature: old things are passed away; behold, all things are become new."* 2 Corinthians 5:17

Book Study: Joel

> ***Prophetic Word:*** *Quit wasting time on unnecessary and invaluable things that are producing no fruit. Instead of having a desire to be right, it is time to do right. There are answers to your dilemmas, but stop pointing fingers and placing blame. You cannot mandate morality for others, but you can stand up for righteousness yourself. It's you that have moved, not Me. Return unto Me, says the Lord. You have lowered the standard and dropped your guard then wondered why things are progressively headed downward. I am bringing change to your state, and it's beginning in Springfield and heading towards Chicago. Work with Me, and know I have your best interests in My mind at all times. You won't like all the changes, but after your initial resistances, just remember My words, return to Me. Partner with churches that have leaders who don't have political ambition but have My heart to bring about change. Some of the*

change will come from unusual sources, but be careful not to reject those who I have sent. There will be political scandals revealed in every form and level of government, but I am only sending a shaking to bring you back to a foundation that leads you closer to Me.

Capital: Springfield
Key Month: June
Pray For: Spiritual Receptivity

Indiana

Scripture: *"Heaviness in the heart of man maketh it stoop: but a good word maketh it glad."* Proverbs 12:25

Book Study: Joshua

> ***Prophetic Word:*** *I am continuing the national spotlight upon your state in 2017. Don't settle for your 15 minutes of fame and rest on your laurels. I have not called you to win a round, but I have called you to win the fight. Don't score a run and think because you're ahead, that the game is over. You must fight until the end. Don't settle for fitting in and being average. When you settle for average, you're just as far from the top*

as you are the bottom. Your measuring stick for victory cannot be defeating the enemy, but destroying the enemy. I need you to listen to the details, and follow the instruction without changing the original intent of My message. You're going to have to care more than others think is smart and risk more than others think is safe. Ultimately, you will have a deeper appreciation of the view when you get to the top, because you have been willing to pay the price, and make the sacrifice to climb, instead of settling at a lower altitude. Thursdays are your God-days, so look for mercy and grace to catch up with you.

Capital: Indianapolis
Key Month: April
Pray For: A willingness to do right with a good attitude

Iowa

Scripture: *"Death and life are in the power of the tongue: and they that love it shall eat the fruit thereof."* Proverbs 18:21

Book Study: Isaiah

Prophetic Word: *Watch what you say, and be careful how you speak. Your words will determine what direction you head toward in 2017 and beyond. What you allow and participate in now, will have a lasting effect. What you sow is what you reap. Sow a thought, reap an action. Sow an action, reap a habit. Sow a habit, reap a character. Sow a character, reap a destiny. Thoughts determine your destiny. What you think on long enough will eventually come out of your mouth. You are what you speak. Sanitize your mouth with the water of My Word. Don't blame Me, the devil, or others if you don't receive; it's on YOU!!! I am laying before you an open Heaven, so think before you speak, and remember the consequences to help keep you on the right track. Your giants are not too big to hit, they are too big to miss. Call it forth in Jesus name.*

Capital: Des Moines
Key Month: August
Pray For: Guarding your mouth

Kansas

Scripture: *"But ye, beloved, building up yourselves on your most holy faith, praying in the Holy Ghost,"* Jude v.20

Book Study: Romans

Prophetic Word: I have given you life, but I desire for you to live alive. Many times you have been as zombies, so I'm releasing a new level of My spirit upon you throughout the state. It will help in giving you the mind of Christ that is necessary to free you from your past and to have power over sin. You need to die to your selfish desires, and be in right standing with Me. I am breathing new life into you, and I am stirring your spirit to help you understand Me, so you can fulfill your purpose. I need you to be a testimony to the lost, and testify of My goodness to everyone you come into contact with. You are a key state in the center of America that I want to use to start the fire of revival. Topeka, step up, and take the lead in obeying My Word. The winter months are your launching pad, so shoot for the stars, and fish on the right side of the boat.

Capital: Topeka
Key Month: January
Pray For: The power of the Holy Spirit to be activated

Kentucky

Scripture: *"Who shall separate us from the love of Christ? shall tribulation, or distress, or persecution, or famine, or nakedness, or peril, or sword?"* Romans 8:35

Book Study: Judges

> ***Prophetic Word:** My command to love others is not a suggestion that you can refuse. I am calling you to a new level of sacrificial love where you willingly give up something for the benefit of someone. Love is active, not inactive. Love gives and forgives. It can also be uncomfortable because it's easier to hate than to love. I want you to love on purpose, and premeditate love towards others. Be deliberate in your positive behavior and actions. Many situations will arise to test your love walk in 2017, but be committed to work hard, and fulfill your commitment to walk without offense, and love without*

conditions. Summer season is blessing time, so prepare your heart in obedience for the harvest.

Capital: Frankfort
Key Month: December
Pray For: Love and Acceptance

Louisiana

Scripture: *"The Lord is gracious, and full of compassion; slow to anger, and of great mercy."* Psalm 145:8

Book Study: Acts

> ***Prophetic Word:*** *The momentum is shifting, and the tide is turning in your favor. My approval is upon you, and one sign of confirmation will be that I will shower you with My kindness. I am considering conventional and unconventional ways to bless you with My generosity. I have a compassion for you that is beyond a natural sorrow that will result in Me moving to action on your behalf. Stay humble, and know this is because of My grace and not because of your good deeds. I want more from you, so speak up for those whose voices have been silenced. Don't be*

intimidated or allow threats to stop you from doing right in My eyes. Watch your bodies of water for contamination, and don't let your guard down with your security at airports and train stations.

Capital: Baton Rouge
Key Month: February
Pray For: Courage and Strength

Maine

Scripture: *"The steps of a good man are ordered by the Lord: and he delighteth in his way."* Psalm 37:23

Book Study: 1 Thessalonians

> ***Prophetic Word:*** *I brought order out of chaos in the beginning, and I will do the same as the end of time approaches. It is so important that you, above others, do all things decently and in order. I am calling you to treat others with fairness, and live a life where the pieces fit together in a proper way. I don't want you disjointed, disorganized, and disillusioned. I want you fertile, productive, and increasing in wisdom. You must be fruitful before I begin to multiply because if this gets out of order,*

you will only multiply the unfruitfulness. I will help you to correct your priorities as you pursue Me with your heart. Fall has to be a time you are conscious and aware of surroundings, so don't get lost in the moment. Keep an eye on the waters in late summer.

Capital: Augusta
Key Month: April
Pray For: Faithfulness and Fruitfulness

Maryland

Scripture: *"But take heed lest by any means this liberty of yours become a stumbling block to them that are weak."* 1 Corinthians 8:9

Book Study: 3 John

***Prophetic Word:** Some messes are created by bad decisions that have been made in your past. You have felt pressured and rushed to give answers that have only gotten you into trouble. At times you have been self-absorbed and done your own thing without considering the consequences. You have also moved forward and forced things into existence without allowing peace to rule your heart. You have chased after worldly* *pleasures and have not sought My will. I am not saying this to reprimand you but to declare that I'm bigger than your mistakes and bad decisions. I can bring good out of every kind of bad in life even when it's been self-inflicted. I will use your bad decisions as a stepping stone to reverse the curse as you learn and quit repeating your mistakes. Allow Me to remove stubbornness and rebellion from your behavior. Go to My Word to get advice that will help support your decisions. I will not contradict Myself, so don't do anything unless there is written Biblical evidence to prove your case.*

Capital: Annapolis
Key Month: May
Pray For: Better decision-making ability

Massachusetts

Scripture: *"He that committeth sin is of the devil; for the devil sinneth from the beginning. For this purpose the Son of God was manifested, that he might destroy the works of the devil."* 1 John 3:8

Book Study: 1 Kings

> ***Prophetic Word:*** *I will reveal all secret things that are not done to bring My father*

glory. Big scandals will surface in late spring/early summer that will make national news and shock the world. Terrorist's cells and racist hate groups will be exposed before horrible damage can be done. I'm also serving a challenge to My godly warriors in this state to declare war against witchcraft, but fight it on your knees in the spiritual realm. You will have to combine your prayer with fasting to experience the ultimate success. All battles are won in the spiritual before they manifest in the natural. There are Elijah's among you, but judge them by the fruit of My Word, so you don't allow weirdness and a spirit of err to deceive you. Your weapons are not carnal but mighty through the Lord.

Capital: Boston
Key Month: June
Pray For: Breaking the power of all demonic bondage

Michigan

Scripture: *"I have fought a good fight, I have finished my course, I have kept the faith:"* 2 Timothy 4:7

Book Study: Micah

> ***Prophetic Word:*** *Don't allow the unacceptable to become legal. There are fights to fight in the coming days, so don't allow a lack of resources to be a reason you stop the pursuit of holding up a standard of righteousness. Don't grow weary in well doing and allow the enemy to rob you of your joy while going through the process. It's easy for Me to fix this, but it's more about what I want to do inside of you than what I want to do for you. This is your lion and your bear, but Goliath is yet to come. Do the small things great, and prove your willingness and your desire to obey. Your friends comfort you, but your enemies have the ability to bring promotion your way. Wait, watch, and continue to work, so I can give you the victory and make the devil pay for it.*

Capital: Lansing
Key Month: September
Pray For: Ability to finish the race

Minnesota

Scripture: *"Repent ye therefore, and be converted, that your sins may be blotted out, when the times of refreshing shall come from the presence of the Lord."* Acts 3:19

Book Study: 1 Timothy

Prophetic Word: *A spirit of anti-Christ is upon the state. You have ridden the fence and given the enemy an open door through compromise. He has taken more ground than you ever intended. There have been many imposters, seducers, and deceivers that have led you astray, but you have willingly followed. Stop running ahead of My will. Quit looking for signs in the sky that will only continue to mislead you. You have allowed others to be given a place in your heart that is reserved for Me. You have suppressed and disturbed My people and resisted Me. There is still time! Heed the call! Open your eyes, and acknowledge your sin. I will forgive and cleanse you. I will also allow you to recapture the former glory of My spirit, and experience the reality of My presence upon your repentance. Double check every point of separation. Discern spirits that rule when crossing bridges,* *railroad tracks, rivers, county lines, etc. I am with you!!!*

Capital: St. Paul
Key Month: July
Pray For: Repentance and Discernment

Mississippi

Scripture: *"Have not I commanded thee? Be strong and of a good courage; be not afraid, neither be thou dismayed: for the Lord thy God is with thee whithersoever thou goest."* Joshua 1:9

Book Study: Jeremiah

> ***Prophetic Word:*** *The missing and lost will be found. The hunt is on, and the whereabouts of what has been taken shall soon be discovered. You have searched and become discouraged because you have not found. You have even looked in the right places, but have not looked at the obvious. Look again, and see what's right in front of you instead of looking for the abstract. It's been right there all the time. Great joy will come when you seek and search because this time you will find what you have been looking and longing for to be returned*

Capital: Jackson
Key Month: July
Pray For: Recovery and Discovery

Missouri

Scripture: *"Call unto me, and I will answer thee, and show thee great and mighty things, which thou knowest not."* Jeremiah 33:3

Book Study: Ruth

> ***Prophetic Word:*** *Never allow great loss to go unresolved because it can cause bitterness. Bitterness is when anger and resentment enter your hearts because situations are hard to accept and/or it takes too long to change. Remember Naomi!!! She was a perfect wife and an awesome mom, but tragedy struck as she lost them all in war. The more she remembered what she lost, the more depressed she became. Bitterness caused her judgment to become impaired, and it even began to change her appearance. Bitterness will convince you that your problems don't have solutions. I want to heal you from the inside out, and exchange the bitter things of this world, with the fresh things of God. Don't be poisoned, and always check the dates on perishable*

items. I will protect, but don't neglect the power that is found in using godly wisdom.

Capital: Jefferson City
Key Month: August
Pray For: Godly Wisdom

Montana

Scripture: *"Be not hasty in thy spirit to be angry: for anger resteth in the bosom of fools."* Ecclesiastes 7:9

Book Study: Ezekiel

> ***Prophetic Word:*** *Your spiritual landscape needs to be an object of your concern. Your serious attention is required to change the atmosphere and attitude of My people. Your attitude will determine your altitude, so fix things, so you can ride high with Me. Some things need to be pruned; other things need to be purged and cut off altogether. This is not just a cutting back, or getting rid of things that I desire for you, but I want you to plant in the garden of your heart godly things that will yield a godly harvest. The enemy has been fighting, but your natural commodities are great. Use what you have in your house, and watch a miracle come*

forth. Don't pout or doubt. Look up and not down. This year is a harvest season for those who prune, purge, and plant the good things of God. Also, remember what's at the top has a way of effecting everything below.

Capital: Helena
Key Month: November
Pray For: Harvest Time

Nebraska

Scripture: *"Blessed is the man that endureth temptation: for when he is tried, he shall receive the crown of life, which the Lord hath promised to them that love him."* James 1:12

Book Study: Amos

> ***Prophetic Word:*** *You are to continue to work in the fields, but I'm pulling some of you out to put you on the front lines. Learn your responsibilities, and man your post. Do your job, and allow others to do theirs without trying to tell them how to do it. Don't deviate from My plan or your job description. If all of you work together, your state will become a breeding ground for miracles. Moses went to the mountain to pray, while Joshua fought in the valley.*

Aaron and Hur supported the whole operation. They sought after a God-agenda, not a personal agenda. Stop caring who gets the credit, and know you have been called to do your job better than anyone else. There are no big "I's" or little "U's" in the kingdom of God. You are not in competition with your brothers and sisters in Christ. Work together! Win together!

Capital: Lincoln
Key Month: March
Pray For: Divine Unity

Nevada

Scripture: *"If ye endure chastening, God dealeth with you as with sons; for what son is he whom the father chasteneth not? But if ye be without chastisement, whereof all are partakers, then are ye bastards, and not sons."* Hebrews 12:7-8

Book Study: Ephesians

***Prophetic Word:** Attract My attention for the right reasons in 2017. I'm watching you, but sometimes it's for all the wrong reasons. Your character is what will move My hand in your direction. Pursue a spirit of godly* *excellence within My gates. It is only established through hard work and dedication. Be modest and God-fearing in your behavior. Learn to be frugal, and save instead of spending everything that comes in. I know I ask a hard thing, but I'm not asking too much. It's not beyond your ability to achieve, but discipline is the key to your long-term success. I'm also dealing with entertainers within your borders, so pray their hearts will be turned, so their gifts can be used for MY GLORY.*

Capital: Carson City
Key Month: October
Pray For: Discipline

New Hampshire

Scripture: *"A false balance is abomination to the Lord: but a just weight is his delight."* Proverbs 11:1

Book Study: Jonah

> ***Prophetic Word:*** *You are little in size but great in power. You had a mighty impact on the election last year. Awesome things can come from small places. Small things do matter, but don't let the little things bother*

you so much. Stay steady. Stay balanced. Shake things off quicker, and don't allow them to affect you so long. I am praying for meekness to cover you in 2017, so hurts and troubles slide off instead of sticking to your mind. Let things roll off sooner, and always walk in forgiveness. Put on the armor of God every day. Be prepared for battle, and fight the enemy through prayer. Things are not as difficult as you make them out to be, for nothing is too hard for Me. Watch for summer to bring a spiritual awakening.

Capital: Concord
Key Month: May
Pray For: Balance and Steadiness

New Jersey

Scripture: *"And God looked upon the earth, and, behold, it was corrupt; for all flesh had corrupted his way upon the earth."* Genesis 6:12

Book study: 2 Timothy

> **Prophetic Word:** *There is promotion that will come to your political leaders. Some good will take place throughout the state in 2017. But, make no mistake about it, a revealing of corruption, and an unveiling of*

plots, will dominate the headlines. I am calling My remnant within these borders to a higher level of prayer and fasting. Gluttony in every form has ruled this land, so now is the time to repent, regroup, and have Me help you rewrite some things. You have welcomed and even celebrated a host of demonic activity that is catching up with you. However, all hope is not lost if you hurry to obey. It took a long time to get in this mess, and it won't be fixed overnight, but the process can begin as soon as you want. You can have as much good and God as you want, but it's your choice!!! Let's see what you're made of.

Capital: Trenton
Key Month: April
Pray For: Hope and Joy

New Mexico

Scripture: *"Grace and peace be multiplied unto you through the knowledge of God, and of Jesus our Lord, According as his divine power hath given unto us all things that pertain unto life and godliness, through the knowledge of him that hath called us to glory and virtue: Whereby are given unto us exceeding great and precious promises:*

that by these ye might be partakers of the divine nature, having escaped the corruption that is in the world through lust." 2 Peter 1:2-4

Book Study: Zephaniah

> ***Prophetic Word:*** *I am bothered more by the absence of good than by the presence of evil within your state. The evil is great with witchcraft, the occult, and unnatural affections leading the way. I am saddened by the lack of effort put into making things "good". I am calling you to wake up out of your spiritual slumber and put your hands to the plow. Laziness and apathy have increased over the past four years, while your discernment has decreased. Be influenced by the right things, and don't seek approval from those whose motives are wrong. Put effort into caring for yourselves in the natural, spiritual, and emotional areas of your life. Look for scandals in reservations to make national news and bring a spotlight to your state in 2017.*

Capital: Santa Fe
Key Month: November
Pray For: Refreshing of body, soul, and spirit

New York

Scripture: *"Moreover the law entered, that the offence might abound. But where sin abounded, grace did much more abound:"* Romans 5:20

Book Study: James

> **Prophetic Word:** *The mask of hypocrisy will be lifted, and wow, will it be a surprise to most people! It will cause a shaking that can be used to bring you closer to Me. Trouble is coming, but don't be afraid or dismayed. You're used to it, but you're tired of it as well. It's all going to be ok, but there are more tough times you will have to endure. Don't allow a demonic stronghold to enter your mindset and impregnate it with hopelessness. Continue to bounce back, and stand up. Near Buffalo there is an important place to watch for unholy connections. New voices will be lifted up from this city that gained public notice. Look for huge news from Wall Street in the first part of October that affects the world. Shifting, shaking, and shocking news will come from your land in 2017.*

Capital: Albany
Key Month: January
Pray For: Determination and Tenacity

North Carolina

Scripture: *"The meek also shall increase their joy in the Lord, and the poor among men shall rejoice in the Holy One of Israel."* Isaiah 29:19

Book Study: Haggai

> ***Prophetic Word:*** *Your influence is growing throughout the land and will continue to increase in 2017. You have been given a voice to speak, and others are listening. Use your platform wisely. Whatever you have lost as a result of your decisions shall be replaced. Medical advances will come from your state. Pay attention for new discoveries to be released that will encourage those sick in this world. A champion will arise among you and shall be crowned as the greatest. Elevation, promotion, and advancement is yours, so embrace it while the heavens are open over you.*

Capital: Raleigh
Key Month: December
Pray For: Increase and favor from the Lord

North Dakota

Scripture: *"I called upon the Lord in distress: the Lord answered me, and set me in a large place."* Psalm 118:5

Book Study: Zechariah

> ***Prophetic Word:*** *Protect your border to the North from unsavory characters with bad intentions. They are looking for new avenues to enter the country, and you must be attentive. Don't drop the ball or let your guard down. Be discreet in your searching, and be ok with being the unknown heroes of the nation. Remain faithful knowing it's your insurance policy for the future. David was faithful in the fields, Abigail was faithful to a foolish man, and Paul was faithful in prison. They all got their reward and so shall you. Store up a little more, for winter hits twice.*

Capital: Bismarck
Key Month: March
Pray For: Godly discretion and insight

Ohio

Scripture: *"And ye shall know the truth, and the truth shall make you free."* John 8:32

Book Study: Esther

Prophetic Word: You are the 17th state, and it is more than just luck of the draw as you were meant to be in the limelight for such a time as this. You will be at the center of attention throughout the United States in 2017. Some reasons will be for your past mistakes, and some reasons will be for your future endeavors. I am releasing a creative spirit over the state; however, be careful how you use this God-given power. Look for scientists to claim they have discovered cures for certain diseases. Keep your eyes upon the universities in the state as they will be releasing information in spring and fall that can be used to generate prosperity throughout the nation as their truths are applied. You will also be given the ability to rewrite and correct things that have been written in error from the past. Don't reject or accept anything until you judge it according to My Word. If it holds up to the standard that I have laid forth in My Word, then embrace it with your whole heart. Rough weather is ahead, and some turbulence is above, but I am with you. Pay attention to the key dates for 2017 because there is great significance and secret messages that I will want to relay to you.

Capital: Columbus
Key Month: Every month
Pray For: Gifts of the Spirit to be in operation daily

Oklahoma

Scripture: *"And it shall come to pass in the last days, saith God, I will pour out of my Spirit upon all flesh: and your sons and your daughters shall prophesy, and your young men shall see visions, and your old men shall dream dreams:"* Acts 2:17

Book Study: Habakkuk

> ***Prophetic Word:*** *If at first you don't succeed, try again. This is a year where things will work that haven't worked in the past. Don't allow past failures to stop you from pursuing your dreams. Don't put on people now what other people have done to you previously. This is a new day, so embrace it for what it is. The timing is right, and My will is now. Discouragement has*

crept in, but let faith arise. This time you will succeed. Never allow your past defeats to get in the way of future victories. There will also be major discoveries in the ground that will produce prosperity, so watch while you work. This a year to seize possession, and take pleasure in My presence.

Capital: Oklahoma City
Key Month: June
Pray For: Trust in God and divine connections with people

Oregon

Scripture: *"And thou shalt love the Lord thy God with all thine heart, and with all thy soul, and with all thy might."* Deuteronomy 6:5

Book Study: Deuteronomy

> ***Prophetic Word:*** *I have given you a peace that passes all understanding, but you have to receive it. Stop rejecting My gifts, and know that I have given them to you to help you live victoriously. Stop forfeiting the peace I have provided for you by allowing what you see to create doubt inside your heart. Walk in faith and not fear. Fear is stifling your growth and holding you back*

from walking into your destiny. It is false evidence that appears real, but never allow your perception to outweigh spiritual reality. Trust Me and know I will give you the strength to overcome in every area of your life, both physically and emotionally, as well as politically and personal; whether you're single or married, male or female, look up, for your redemption draws nigh. There are challenges ahead, so look for the earth to split, the ground to open, and the sky to reveal signs that will make you wonder during the year, but keep your eyes upon Me. Put business transactions off to the spring, and don't be in a hurry to say yes to something that I'm wanting you to wait on in order to prefect for your good.

Capital: Salem
Key Month: September
Pray For: Endurance and Faith

Pennsylvania

Scripture: *"Wherefore we labour, that, whether present or absent, we may be accepted of him."* 2 Corinthians 5:9

Book Study: Matthew

Prophetic Word: *There is a sense of great frustration that has entered the heart of the church. A deep annoyance and anger has been an emotional response to friend and foe alike. It's time to deal with your negative emotions that infected you and affected others. I know you feel like you have little strength, but now is the time for complete dependence upon My Word. Keep the faith, and walk patiently, and I will make those who have opposed you to redirect their attacks. Run through the door to worship Me, and find your place of rest. Not much time remains, so continue to be an overcomer, and hold your head high. Pittsburgh and Philadelphia have been resistant, but the center of the state is spreading its witness to pierce the darkness. Continue to work, and make no apologies for your godly passion.*

Capital: Harrisburg
Key Month: October
Pray For: Long-Suffering

Rhode Island

Scripture: *"By humility and the fear of the Lord are riches, and honour, and life."* Proverbs 22:4

Book Study: Proverbs

Prophetic Word: *The key to your blessing in 2017 is in relation to your ability to fear and respect the Lord. Discontentment has flooded your borders, and you haven't hated evil as I require. Pride and arrogance have been bushes you have hid behind to avoid dealing with issues that need resolution. I am releasing a new sense of awareness of My awesomeness. It's designed to bring you back and help you understand how important it is to respect My commands. Satisfaction, riches, and a prolonging of your days will be your reward. I will also give you a sense of security that will calm your nerves and free you from worrying about impending danger. Be extra protective in mid-summer.*

Capital: Providence
Key Month: June
Pray For: A greater respect for God

South Carolina

Scripture: *"For God giveth to a man that is good in his sight wisdom, and knowledge, and joy: but to the sinner he giveth travail, to gather and to* *heap up, that he may give to him that is good before God. This also is vanity and vexation of spirit."* Ecclesiastes 2:26

Book Study: 1 Peter

> ***Prophetic Word:*** *Be determined to rejoice regardless of what comes your way. I am obligated to save you and deliver you from your troubles. Learn to rejoice before the manifestation. Have faith, and hold Me to My Word. When you walk, make it time for us to talk. When you drive, please shut out the distractions, and listen to Me. I want to show you another side of My glory. I want all forms of personal religious practices to be challenged, so you're pliable in My hands. I want to teach you new things, but you can't handle them if you continue to hold on and embrace the old things. They were good yesterday, but today is a new day. I desire to release a joy that will be so contagious it will spread straight across the nation. Also, don't ignore the storm warnings this time. As much as it's against your nature.... Leave. Rejoice in all things!!!*

Capital: Columbia
Key Month: January
Pray For: The ability to rejoice in crisis

South Dakota

Scripture: *"But my God shall supply all your need according to his riches in glory by Christ Jesus."* Philippians 4:19

Book Study: Titus

> ***Prophetic Word:** I am breaking a spirit of strife and discord among people, families, and churches. All fault finding, complaining, arguing, and mean-spiritedness must be replaced with godly love and mutual trust. Seek peace, not war in 2017. All your strife has caused a double-minded nature to occur within you. Fickleness and flip-flopping are not a part of My character. A double-minded man is unstable in everything in his life. Allow Me to fix hearts and mend relationships, so you can know two are way better than one. Also, protect and restore landmarks. Take good care of your natural resources.*

Capital: Pierre
Key Month: September
Pray For: Love and Trust

Tennessee

Scripture: *"And Jabez called on the God of Israel, saying, Oh that thou wouldest bless me indeed, and enlarge my coast, and that thine hand might be with me, and that thou wouldest keep me from evil, that it may not grieve me! And God granted him that which he requested."* 1 Chronicles 4:10

Book Study: Revelation

__Prophetic Word:__ Your present exists with your permission. If you don't like what you're getting, then stop allowing it to continue. Your tolerance is willingly giving it an endorsement to remain. The first three months of 2017 are crucial for your favor to remain throughout the rest of the year. You will be in the spotlight, so maintain your godly standard. Get rid of those things and people that are holding you back and keeping you from walking in your destiny. Everyone won't embrace your God-given purpose. Some will be jealous, and others will feel uncomfortable in your pursuit of Me. Don't overthink, just respond in obedience. Don't consult the logic of your mind to decide your destiny. I reveal piece by piece, so take steps, not leaps, but always *know you will never progress beyond your last act of disobedience. Remove and replace for revival to come.*

Capital: Nashville
Key Month: May
Pray For: Revival and Integrity

Texas

Scripture: *"Casting down imaginations, and every high thing that exalteth itself against the knowledge of God, and bringing into captivity every thought to the obedience of Christ;"* 2 Corinthians 10:5

Book Study: 1 Samuel

> ***Prophetic Word:*** *Some things are hard to understand and reconcile. The more you try and figure them out, the more confused you can become. Bad things happen to good people, and good things happen to bad people. You are wasting your time and creating a greater level of frustration within your state because you're spending time seeking answers to questions that don't exist at this time. Answers may come later, but forcing things won't bring them about*

sooner. It can only cause more problems and increase the handicaps you're already dealing with. Focus in on what is at hand and the answers that are available now. I've answered "no" and "wait" to things in the past but there are things I'm saying, "yes" to as well. Learn to deal in the present. My name is not "I was" or "I will be", My name is "I AM". I am an ever present help in your time of trouble, so reach out to Me, and see with your own eyes if I will not move Heaven and Earth to come to your rescue. San Antonio is key to the technology advancements throughout the state and nation. Also, look for extraordinary large drug seizures to occur in all points of main entry into your state.

Capital: Austin
Key Month: December
Pray For: Walking in the present instead of past or future

Utah

Scripture: *"Be not carried about with divers and strange doctrines. For it is a good thing that the heart be established with grace; not with meats,* *which have not profited them that have been occupied therein."* Hebrews 13:9

Book Study: Hosea

> ***Prophetic Word:*** *Look for the unusual and unique to dominate the headlines in 2017. Things that have never happened, and things that haven't happened in a long time, are going to be a reoccurring theme for your state. I am also expecting unusual and unique things from My church; don't settle for the status quo. Be willing to challenge the system, and be a voice and not an echo. Don't become a spiritual pawn or puppet. Speak up, and speak out without fear of what man can impose upon you. Let this be your finest hour in conquering personal and corporate giants. As I gave David, I also give you five stones: Love, worship, faith, prayer, and My word, so go win the battle and conquer the giant.*

Capital: Salt Lake City
Key Month: February
Pray For: Using the weapons of your warfare to overcome all things

Vermont

Scripture: *"What? know ye not that your body is the temple of the Holy Ghost which is in you, which ye have of God, and ye are not your own?"* 1 Corinthians 6:19

Book Study: Ezra

> *Prophetic Word: I want you to pay attention to your body in 2017. From everything that you eat and put in your system, to the body language you express should be under scrutiny this year. You are a spirit with a body, not a body with a spirit; however, your body has had a negative impact upon your spirit. Your reactions have offended others, and your appetite has made you sluggish. I need your energy level increased as well as I want your influence with others to grow. You must cooperate, and stop making excuses. This is a crucial time to implement the plans that have been sitting dormant for success awaiting your action. Spring is your important season, but be busy about the Father's business all year long.*

Capital: Montpelier
Key Month: July
Pray For: Health and healing in every realm

Virginia

Scripture: *"Yea doubtless, and I count all things but loss for the excellency of the knowledge of Christ Jesus my Lord: for whom I have suffered the loss of all things, and do count them but dung, that I may win Christ,"* Philippians 3:8

Book Study: Hebrews

> ***Prophetic Word:*** *Stress, worry, guilt, doubt, and defeat have entered your gates. You need to cultivate a greater sense of humor to handle tough situations, and change the atmosphere of your state. Practice smiling, and learn to laugh to generate a greater level of quality of life. Show a higher degree of enthusiastic behavior about things that matter the most. I'm turning your negative prospective into a positive one, but work with Me. Let your hair down, and find ways to have fun without entering into compromise. Spend time with those who matter the most, and step out in faith, and try something different. Don't be so judgmental, and respect the opinions of others. Doing these things is the beginning of a return of supernatural joy being released upon you.*

Capital: Richmond
Key Month: November
Pray For: Generating a sense of humor

Washington

Scripture: *"But life is worth nothing unless I use it for doing the work assigned me by the Lord Jesus—the work of telling others the Good News about God's mighty kindness and love."* Acts 20:24 (TLB)

Book Study: Ecclesiastes

> ***Prophetic Word:*** *A year of nostalgia awaits. I am taking you back to fix some things in order to thrust you forward. I am also reconnecting you with people from your past. Some are for personal reasons, and some are God-Sends you rejected that I'm giving you a second chance to join forces. Your immaturity and pride got in the way, so humble yourselves this time, and receive. I am helping you in defining your message and your mission while also correcting your motives. Your contribution in 2017 is measured and is in direct relation to the quality of your character. Go back, and use*

what worked in the past. Couple that with what you have recently learned. Then, allow a marriage to happen between the old and the new that will bring open doors from above. The second winter will be hardest, but you will be victorious.

Capital: Olympia
Key Month: March
Pray For: A spiritual maturity, openness, and receptivity to abide

West Virginia

Scripture: *"Now we exhort you, brethren, warn them that are unruly, comfort the feebleminded, support the weak, be patient toward all men."* 1 Thessalonians 5:14

Book Study: 1 Corinthians

> ***Prophetic Word:*** *As David learned to minister to others when he was in need, I am calling you to do the same. It's hard to give when you're in need, and you have never been in a time of greater need, but don't look within; begin to look without to resolve every difficulty. The answer is inside of you, but the outreach must begin outside your*

borders. Whatever you selflessly make happen for others, I will make happen for you. Doing nothing brings more of the same, but outreach is not just your key to survival, but revival. The hidden natural resources abound in this, and your outreach will allow connections to be developed that will help you make a discovery that can be eternally prosperous. Your original intent should be to reach out without selfish motives, but your obedience will bring blessing.

Capital: Charleston
Key Month: May
Pray For: Selfless behavior to rule the hearts of people

Wisconsin

Scripture: *"And Stephen, full of faith and power, did great wonders and miracles among the people."* Acts 6:8

Book Study: 2 Thessalonians

> ***Prophetic Word:*** *You are the John the Baptist of America. You are called to be the forerunner to lead the way and leave a fiery trail for others to follow. So, run Wisconsin,*

run. Always seek the approval of God before seeking the applause of man. You had other plans, and in time I will allow those to come to pass, but I have you right where I want you. They go by different names, but you have some spiritual Stephens among you. They are people that are full of grace and the power of the Holy Spirit. Study Stephen in Acts, so you are knowledgeable when you come into direct contact with them or hear of their exploits. These people are not afraid to declare the truth and take a stand even if it cost them their life. Quit trying to save your life, and lose it in Me. Abandon yourself to proclaiming the truth and setting the table for My soon return. You won't always be appreciated by others, but remember, your reward is in Heaven, not on this earth.

Capital: Madison
Key Month: October
Pray For: Leadership skills to be enhanced

Wyoming

Scripture: *"I know thy works, that thou art neither cold nor hot: I would thou wert cold or hot. So then because thou art lukewarm, and neither* *cold nor hot, I will spue thee out of my mouth."* Revelation 3:15-16

Book Study: Malachi

> ***Prophetic Word:*** *You have been forgotten by others but never forgotten by Me. I watch and see everything. Good and bad, right and wrong. I know when you're riding the fence of compromise. Choose a side in 2017, and stick with it. Don't be persuaded and easily change your mind. Be hot or be cold, but don't be lukewarm. Stop trying to please others who have no ability to decide your future. Be determined to take up the Cross, and follow Me. Don't be ashamed, and stop being double-minded. I want to matter more to you, so come away with Me. Make your time with Me unequaled in comparison to the time you spend on other things, and the results will be obvious to everyone. Great discoveries will be made in spring.*

Capital: Cheyenne
Key Month: April
Pray For: The fire of God to be ignited in the heart of the people

God is on America's side in 2017. Take these words, and use them to warn, reveal, and encourage you throughout the year. There is a resetting going on in every state, so look for the old to end and new things to begin. The spiritual odometer is going back to zero, and we are getting a second chance to undo the wrong and make things right. Closure is coming while, at the same time, God is laying a new open door before us. Let's take advantage of this once-in-a-lifetime opportunity that the Lord has laid before us, and go, and fulfill our destiny.

CHAPTER IX

Characteristics of People Born on the 17th Day

If you were born on the 17th day of any month, you will find this chapter particularly interesting. There really are specific characteristics that attach themselves to people born on a certain day of a month. Here are just a few:

- Possessive
- Independent
- Self-control
- High energy
- Born leaders
- Domineering
- Original
- Determined
- Addictive personalities
- Anger issues
- Talkative
- Suspicious
- Offensive
- Creative
- Risk-takers
- Make great politicians and entertainers
- False compassion

- Sound in judgment
- Distrusting
- Serious

Famous People Born on the 17th Day of the Month

January 17th

Muhammad Ali - Boxer
Dwayne Wade – NBA
Jim Carrey – Actor
Michelle Obama – First Lady
Andy Kaufman – Actor
Betty White – Actress
Al Capone – Criminal
James Earl Jones – Actor
Benjamin Franklin – Scientist
Robert F. Kennedy Jr. – Politician
Steve Harvey – Actor
Lil Jon – Music Producer
Kid Rock – Singer
Steve Earle – Musician
Vidal Sassoon – Hair Care Professional

February 17th

Ed Sheeran – Musician
Michael Jordan – NBA
Lou Diamond Phillips – Actor
Paris Hilton – Celebrity

Jim Brown – NFL
Larry the Cable Guy – Comedian

March 17th

Rob Lowe – Actor
Nat King Cole – Singer
Mia Hamm – Soccer
Kurt Russell – Actor
Gary Sinise – Actor

April 17th

Victoria Beckham – Model/singer
Jennifer Garner – Actress
J.P. Morgan – Business
Georges J.F. Kohler – Scientist

May 17th

Craig Ferguson – Comedian
Sugar Ray Leonard – Boxer
Dennis Hopper – Actor
Bob Saget – Actor
Derek Jeter – MLB
Maureen O'Sullivan – Actress

June 17th

Venus Williams – Tennis
Will Forte – Actor
Barry Manilow – Singer
Greg Kinnear – Actor
Newt Gingrich – Government Official
Joe Piscopo – Actor

July 17th

Phyllis Diller – Comedian
David Hasselhoff – Actor
Angela Merkel – Chancellor
Camilla Parker Bowles – Duchess
Art Linkletter – Author
James Cagney – Actor
Mark Burnett – TV Producer

August 17th

Donnie Wahlberg – Actor
Gracie Gold – Figure Skater
Belinda Carlisle – Singer
Sean Penn – Actor
Maureen O'Hara – Actress
Robert DeNiro – Actor
Mae West – Actress
Charles I of Austria – Emperor
Charlotte Forten – Civil Rights Activist

September 17th

    Hank Williams – Musician
    Phil Jackson – NBA Coach
    Alex Ovechkin – NHL
    John Ritter – Actor
    Roddy McDowall – Actor
    Warren Burger – Supreme Court Justice
    Anne Bancroft – Actress
    George Blanda – NFL

October 17th

    Eminem – Rapper
    Evel Knievel – Stuntman
    Arthur Miller – Screenwriter
    Rita Hayworth – Dancer, Actress
    George Wendt – Actor
    Ziggy Marley – Musician
    Felicity Jones – Actress
    Montgomery Clift – Actor
    Alan Jackson – Singer

November 17th

    RuPaul – Actor
    John Boehner – Politician
    Danny DeVito – Actor
    Rock Hudson – Actor
    Martin Scorsese – Director
    Lorne Michaels – TV Producer

December 17th

    Sarah Paulson – Actress
    Pope Francis – Religious Leader
    Chris Matthews – Journalist
    Manny Pacquiao – Boxer

Prophetic word for people born on the 17th day of the month

"This is a year that will bring complete closure to an open wound. The mysteries and uncertainty that have been attached to certain relationships will be brought to a conclusion. Things will become clearer. You will have to protect yourself from anger that will arise because things didn't get figured out sooner. You are not a fool by any means. You have to let things go, and never look back. This has been a learning process, and you have grown in the middle of emotional chaos. Don't waste time seeing a door that is being closed. You have not wasted your investment. Turn around, and see the open door of opportunity that I have laid before you. Finances, promotion, and relationships are all yours in 2017 when you let go of your past and begin to RESET your life according to My principles," says the Lord. "Clean your heart, and rid yourself of all toxins that have poisoned your thinking. I AM breathing life into you the way I breathed into Adam. You won't be just living, you will be alive. I AM giving you a renewed energy to complete tasks that have not been finished. I AM giving you the ability to control the habits that have caused you shame. I AM giving you healing from things that have caused you pain. Dare to live again, and be who I have called you to be. You are a voice and not an echo. Be okay with who I have created you to be in this world. Rejoice in your uniqueness. Let go, and let God!!!"

Scripture of the Year for people born on the 17th day

"Sanctify them in the truth [set them apart for Your purposes, make them holy]; Your word is truth." John 17:17 (Amplified)

CHAPTER X

BIBLE BY THE NUMBERS

The Bible was written over a 1,500 year period. It had approximately 40 authors on three continents from different professions including kings, politicians, doctors, fishermen, philosophers, and scholars. It was written in three different languages during times of war and times of peace, in places of chaos, in dungeons, on land, on water, in deserts, mountains, plains, synagogues, and under the stars. The Bible is the best-selling book of all-time with over five billion copies sold and is available in 2,454 languages. When the Bible was first written, it didn't have chapters or verses like today. Stephen Langton is credited with dividing the Bible into chapters around A.D. 1228. The Old Testament was divided into verses by R. Nathan in A.D. 1448, and Robert Stephanus divided the New Testament into verses in A.D. 1551. The first complete Bible with chapter and verse divisions was the Geneva Bible of A.D. 1560.

Interesting Bible Facts

- The Old Testament has 39 books with 23,143 verses
- The New Testament has 27 books with 7,959 verses
- The complete Bible has 66 books with 31,102 verses
- The Old Testament has 592,439 words
- The New Testament has 181,253 words
- The complete Bible has 773,692 words
- The Old Testament has 929 chapters
- The New Testament has 260 chapters
- The complete Bible has 1,189 chapters
- The middle chapter of the Bible is Psalm 118 with the middle verse being 118:8, *"It is better to take refuge in the Lord than to trust in man."*
- The shortest chapter in the Bible is Psalm 117
- The longest chapter in the Bible is Psalm 119
- The shortest book in the Bible is Obadiah
- The longest book in the Bible is Psalms
- The middle book of the Old Testament is Proverbs
- The middle chapter of the Old Testament is Job 20

- The middle verse of the Old Testament is 2 Chronicles 20:17 (scripture of the year)
- The middle book of the New Testament is 1 Thessalonians
- The middle chapter of the New Testament is Romans 8
- The middle verse of the New Testament is Acts 27:17
- The longest verse in the Bible is Esther 8:9 which has 90 words
- The shortest verse in the Bible is John 11:35 which has 2 words

Most Mentioned Men of the Bible
David = 1,118 times
Jesus = 973 times
Moses = 740 times
Aaron = 339 times
Abraham = 306 times

Most Mentioned Women of the Bible
Sarah, Abraham's wife = 57 times
Rachel, Jacob's 2nd wife = 47 times
Leah, Jacob's 1st wife = 34 times
Rebekah, Isaac's wife = 31 times
Jezebel, evil queen = 23 times

- God is personally quoted over 3,000 times in the Bible. All quotes begin with *"Thus saith the Lord"*
- Paul wrote 14 books of the Bible in the New Testament
- Moses wrote five books in the Old testament

The Old Testament has 17 Historical Books:

- Genesis
- Exodus
- Leviticus
- Numbers
- Deuteronomy
- Joshua
- Judges
- Ruth
- 1 Samuel
- 2 Samuel
- 1 Kings
- 2 Kings
- 1 Chronicles
- 2 Chronicles
- Ezra
- Nehemiah
- Esther

The Old Testament has Five Poetic Books:

- Job
- Psalms
- Proverbs
- Ecclesiastes
- Song of Solomon

The Old Testament has 17 Prophetic Books:

- Isaiah
- Jeremiah
- Lamentations
- Ezekiel
- Daniel
- Hosea
- Joel
- Amos
- Obadiah
- Jonah
- Micah
- Nahum
- Habakkuk
- Zephaniah
- Haggai
- Zechariah
- Malachi

The New Testament has Four Gospels:

- Matthew
- Mark
- Luke
- John

The New Testament has One Historical Book:

- Acts

The New Testament has One Prophetic Book:

- Revelation

The New Testament has 21 Epistles:

- Romans
- 1 Corinthians
- 2 Corinthians
- Galatians
- Ephesians
- Philippians
- Colossians
- 1 Thessalonians
- 2 Thessalonians
- 1 Timothy
- 2 Timothy
- Titus
- Philemon
- Hebrews
- James
- 1 Peter
- 2 Peter
- 1 John
- 2 John
- 3 John
- Jude

- The oldest man in the Bible was named Methuselah. He lived to be 969 years old: Genesis 5:27
- Two men in the Bible never died:
    o Enoch in Genesis 5:24, who was Methuselah's dad
    o Elijah in 2 Kings 2:11
- The tallest man in the bible was Goliath, who was 9 ½ feet tall, 1 Samuel 17:4
- Job is the oldest book of the Bible written around 1500 B.C.
- Revelation is the newest book of the Bible written around 95 A.D.

- Esther and Song of Solomon are the only books of the Bible that don't mention the word, "God"
- There are 3,294 questions that are asked in the Bible
- A man's hair weighed 6 ½ pounds in 2 Samuel 14:26
- A man walked naked for three years in Isaiah 20:2-3

Allow these interesting facts to stimulate a desire to research God's Word more in your life in 2017.

CHAPTER XI

SCRIPTURES FOR SUCCESS

All Scriptures with "Seventeen"

Genesis 7:11
*"In the six hundredth year of Noah's life, in the second month, the **seventeen**th day of the month, the same day were all the fountains of the great deep broken up, and the windows of heaven were opened."*

Genesis 8:4
*"And the ark rested in the seventh month, on the **seventeen**th day of the month, upon the mountains of Ararat."*

Genesis 37:2
*"These are the generations of Jacob. Joseph, being **seventeen** years old, was feeding the flock with his brethren; and the lad was with the sons of Bilhah, and with the sons of Zilpah, his father's wives: and Joseph brought unto his father their evil report."*

Genesis 47:28
*"And Jacob lived in the land of Egypt **seventeen** years: so the whole age of Jacob was an hundred forty and seven years."*

Judges 8:14
*"And caught a young man of the men of Succoth, and enquired of him: and he described unto him the princes of Succoth, and the elders thereof, even threescore and **seventeen** men."*

Judges 8:26
*"The weight of the gold rings he asked for came to **seventeen** hundred shekels, not counting the ornaments, the pendants and the purple garments worn by the kings of Midian or the chains that were on their camels' necks."* (NIV)

1 Kings 14:21
*"And Rehoboam the son of Solomon reigned in Judah. Rehoboam was forty and one years old when he began to reign, and he reigned **seventeen** years in Jerusalem, the city which the LORD did choose out of all the tribes of Israel, to put his name there. And his mother's name was Naamah an Ammonitess."*

1 Kings 22:51
*"Ahaziah the son of Ahab began to reign over Israel in Samaria the **seventeen**th year of Jehoshaphat king of Judah, and reigned two years over Israel."*

2 Kings 13:1
*"In the three and twentieth year of Joash the son of Ahaziah king of Judah Jehoahaz the son of Jehu began to reign over Israel in Samaria, and reigned **seventeen** years."*

2 Kings 16:1
*"In the **seventeen**th year of Pekah the son of Remaliah Ahaz the son of Jotham king of Judah began to reign."*

1 Chronicles 7:11
*"All these the sons of Jediael, by the heads of their fathers, mighty men of valour, were **seventeen** thousand and two hundred soldiers, fit to go out for war and battle."*

1 Chronicles 24:15
*"The **seventeen**th to Hezir, the eighteenth to Aphses,"*

1 Chronicles 25:24
*"The **seventeen**th to Joshbekashah, he, his sons, and his brethren, were twelve:"*

1 Chronicles 26:30 (NIV)
*"From the Hebronites: Hashabiah and his relatives – **seventeen** hundred able men – were responsible in Israel west of the Jordan for all the work of the Lord and for the king's service."*

2 Chronicles 12:13
*"So king Rehoboam strengthened himself in Jerusalem, and reigned: for Rehoboam was one and forty years old when he began to reign, and he reigned **seventeen** years in Jerusalem, the city which the LORD had chosen out of all the tribes of Israel, to put his name there. And his mother's name was Naamah an Ammonitess."*

Ezra 2:39
*"The children of Harim, a thousand and **seventeen**."*

Nehemiah 7:42
*"The children of Harim, a thousand and **seventeen**."*

Jeremiah 32:9
*"And I bought the field of Hanameel my uncle's son, that was in Anathoth, and weighed him the money, even **seventeen** shekels of silver."*

Important 20:17 Scriptures

Genesis 20:17
"So Abraham prayed unto God: and God healed Abimelech, and his wife, and his maidservants; and they bare children."

Exodus 20:17
"Thou shalt not covet thy neighbour's house, thou shalt not covet thy neighbour's wife, nor his manservant, nor his maidservant, nor his ox, nor his ass, nor any thing that is thy neighbour's."

Leviticus 20:17
"And if a man shall take his sister, his father's daughter, or his mother's daughter, and see her nakedness, and she see his nakedness; it is a wicked thing; and they shall be cut off in the sight of their people: he hath uncovered his sister's nakedness; he shall bear his iniquity."

Deuteronomy 20:17
"But thou shalt utterly destroy them; namely, the Hittites, and the Amorites, the Canaanites, and the Perizzites, the Hivites, and the Jebusites; as the LORD thy God hath commanded thee:"

1 Samuel 20:17
"And Jonathan caused David to swear again, because he loved him: for he loved him as he loved his own soul."

2 Chronicles 20:17
"Ye shall not need to fight in this battle: set yourselves, stand ye still, and see the salvation of the LORD with you, O Judah and Jerusalem: fear not, nor be dismayed; to morrow go out against them: for the LORD will be with you."

Proverbs 20:17
"Bread of deceit is sweet to a man; but afterwards his mouth shall be filled with gravel."

Jeremiah 20:17
"Because he slew me not from the womb; or that my mother might have been my grave, and her womb to be always great with me."

Luke 20:17
"And he beheld them, and said, What is this then that is written, The stone which the builders rejected, the same is become the head of the corner?"

John 20:17
"Jesus saith unto her, Touch me not; for I am not yet ascended to my Father: but go to my brethren, and say unto them, I ascend unto my Father, and your Father; and to my God, and your God."

17 Scriptures to Meditate on in 2017

Leviticus 25:9
"Then shalt thou cause the trumpet of the jubile to sound on the tenth day of the seventh month, in the day of atonement shall ye make the trumpet sound throughout all your land."

Isaiah 43:18-19
"Remember ye not the former things, neither consider the things of old. Behold, I will do a new thing; now it shall spring forth; shall ye not know it? I will even make a way in the wilderness, and rivers in the desert."

Acts 2:1-4

"And when the day of Pentecost was fully come, they were all with one accord in one place. And suddenly there came a sound from heaven as of a rushing mighty wind, and it filled all the house where they were sitting. And there appeared unto them cloven tongues like as of fire, and it sat upon each of them. And they were all filled with the Holy Ghost, and began to speak with other tongues, as the Spirit gave them utterance."

Ezekiel 37:10

"So I prophesied as he commanded me, and the breath came into them, and they lived, and stood up upon their feet, an exceeding great army."

Isaiah 53:5

"But he was wounded for our transgressions, he was bruised for our iniquities: the chastisement of our peace was upon him; and with his stripes we are healed."

Proverbs 17:17

"A friend loveth at all times, and a brother is born for adversity."

Philippians 2:14
"Do all things without murmurings and disputings:"

Matthew 24:42
"Watch therefore: for ye know not what hour your Lord doth come."

Mark 9:23
"Jesus said unto him, If thou canst believe, all things are possible to him that believeth."

Ephesians 5:14
"Wherefore he saith, Awake thou that sleepest, and arise from the dead, and Christ shall give thee light."

Luke 10:20
"Notwithstanding in this rejoice not, that the spirits are subject unto you; but rather rejoice, because your names are written in heaven."

John 17:17
"Sanctify them through thy truth: thy word is truth."

Obadiah 1:17

"But upon mount Zion shall be deliverance, and there shall be holiness; and the house of Jacob shall possess their possessions."

1 John 1:7

"But if we walk in the light, as he is in the light, we have fellowship one with another, and the blood of Jesus Christ his Son cleanseth us from all sin."

Psalm 133:1

"Behold, how good and how pleasant it is for brethren to dwell together in unity!"

Romans 8:1

"There is therefore now no condemnation to them which are in Christ Jesus, who walk not after the flesh, but after the Spirit."

Revelation 22:13

"I am Alpha and Omega, the beginning and the end, the first and the last."

CHAPTER XII

JOURNAL

Journaling is one way to look back on, and remind us of, the miracle working power of God in our lives. In Matthew 16, Jesus encouraged His disciples to journal and document the miracles they saw in order to remain strong and not lose faith. It's important that we write blessings down and document important dates and events to encourage ourselves when the enemy wants us to forget the greatness of God. This chapter is to log such events. When you hear the number 17 mentioned, document where, when, and why it was mentioned. See if it has any significance to the vision cast out for 2017. You will be surprised by how many times this number is going to pop up when you're paying attention and sensitive to hearing it on TV, radio, newspaper articles, etc. At the end of the year, you will hopefully have a couple sheets of paper to help you judge whether the prophetic message of this book has been relevant in your life and in the world.

Here are the 17 dates the Lord spoke to me to be on the lookout for something:

1. Thursday, January 5, 2017
   _____

2. Friday, January 20, 2017
   _____

3. Wednesday, February 8, 2017
   _____

4. Friday, February 17, 2017
   _____

5. Monday, March 6, 2017
   _____

6. Sunday, April 2, 2017
   _____

7. Tuesday, April 18, 2017
   _____

8. Wednesday, May 3, 2017
   _____

9. Saturday, June 10, 2017

10. Friday, July 7, 2017

11. Monday, August 21, 2017

12. Wednesday, September 13, 2017

13. Friday, September 29, 2017

14. Thursday, October 5, 2017

15. Monday, October 23, 2017

16. Tuesday, November 14, 2017

17. Saturday, December 16, 2017

Date: Comments:

Date: Comments:

Date:	Comments:

CONCLUSION

Generally speaking, every prophetic word must meet the three-fold criteria found in 1 Corinthians 14:3, *"But he that prophesieth speaketh unto men edification, and exhortation, and comfort."*

Three-Fold Purpose of Prophecy

1. **Edify** = to build, establish, and instruct in order to improve.
2. **Exhort** = to advise and strongly urge others to apply knowledge
3. **Comfort** = to ease the grief of another and offer hope

All prophecy must build up others and help lay a foundation for them to improve their lives as they apply the prophetic word. It should also offer hope and ease the pain in someone's heart. The only exception would be if someone has the office gift of Prophet attached to their life. Keep in mind that just because you prophesy, doesn't mean you're a Prophet. The Prophet would be allowed to extend beyond those borders and offer correction. To correct would be to point out some errors and lay out a course of action to avoid punishment. A Prophet edifies, exhorts, comforts, and corrects. The Prophetic Almanac for 2017 is really hitting all four of those areas.

God is provided us with a once-in-a-life time opportunity, not to just bring closure to things in our past, but also to have the ability to start on a level playing field and rewrite the story of our lives. That might sound exciting, but don't forget your cooperation is necessary. God won't do it all. Allow the words of this book to encourage and educate while also helping you to remain conscientious of the warnings God wants us to heed.

God is adjusting and correcting things in our hearts, so be willing to be pliable in His hands, so you can hit the **RESET** button. In doing that, you will be afforded a once-in-a-lifetime opportunity to rewrite the history of your life. Your obedience will release **DIVINE HEALING** in your body and **TOTAL VICTORY** in every area of mind, soul, and spirit. God isn't doing this so we can feel better and be blessed, but for us to shine the light of Jesus Christ to **REVEAL** His will in 2017.

Don't Miss Out!!

www.ingramcontent.com/pod-product-compliance
Lightning Source LLC
Chambersburg PA
CBHW052026070526
44584CB00016B/1920